Dear Tom,

Merry Christmas 2014.

Love Connie and Lee

x x x

amuse-bouche

A tiny taste of heaven

All recipes in this book will make 8 amuse-bouches

unless otherwise stated

Concombre et Boeuf Paquets (page 87)

amuse-bouche

amuse-bouche

Dana Wood and Gillie Bowen

PHOTOGRAPHY Michael Bowen & Dana Wood
ILLUSTRATIONS Aude Kamlet
TRANSLATIONS Claire Eugene
DESIGN Gillie Bowen
Additional photographs by Mike Herringshaw and Gillie Bowen

ACKNOWLEDGEMENTS

With thanks to all our friends for their healthy appetites, copious advice and encouragement. Further thanks to our husbands, Peter and Mike, for their contributions and patience

First published in Great Britain in November 2011 by
Bowood Publishing

Second edition published May 2012

bowoodpublishing@orange.fr

ISBN-13: 978-1467991155

Contents

Introduction

What's an amuse-bouche?

This is a guide to little things that can pop up at the onset or in the middle of a meal at an upmarket restaurant but are not only reserved for that lofty and rarely indulged station.

Amuse-bouche is a French creation and roughly translates into 'taste tantalizer', and more suggestively, 'titillating teaser' or 'palate pleaser'. In some cases, an amuse-bouche can be every bit as delicious and inventive as the best of meals. Their purpose is to introduce exciting, unusual flavours and ingredients in tiny quantities in one or two mouthfuls. Primarily, they are vehicles for the chef's artistry, whimsy and one-upmanship.

Between us, we have lived in the Loire Valley in France for over 20 years. One English, one American, we began to introduce amuse-bouche into our own lunches and dinners. Inevitably an admiring guest suggested: "You should collect these and write a cookbook."

So here it is! In this book we hope to introduce American and British hosts and hostesses to the concept of amuse-bouche.

You might be confused by some of the unfamiliar nomenclature in the recipes as we have frequently discovered the truth of the familiar remark about England and the U.S. being two countries separated by a common language. Every effort has been made to produce recipes that are cook-friendly on both sides of the Atlantic.

Most of the recipes that follow have suggestions on 'presentation' or, in other words, how they are brought to the table. In France a variety of plates, glasses, cups and spoons designed for amuse-bouche can be easily purchased but may not be so available in the U.K. and U.S. But don't let that hold you back. Small saucers, egg cups, liqueur glasses or Chinese soup spoons are good substitutes. Just remember: keep it small. An amuse-bouche is a brief pause in a meal and not a course and can be consumed, without being rude, in a single sip or swallow.

In this book, we also include our version of a 'Trou Normand' which originates from Normandy and should involve an alcoholic spirit. It is served as a palate cleanser between courses.

We hope this book will inspire you to try out your own ideas and recipes. You can create an amuse-bouche from just about anything you've got in the fridge; some lentil, pumpkin or potato soup is perfect; jazz it up with a tiny bit of foie gras in the bottom and top with shreds of sautéed cured meat, pesto or cheese – delicious! The fact is that as long as it's small, tasty and pleasing to the eye, almost anything can make an amuse-bouche.

Some of the amuse-bouches in this book use one of our Store Cupboard/Pantry recipes which can be found on pages 137-141. Make them yourself or buy the equivalent from your local store so that you always have them to hand to prepare a little tingler for the taste buds at the drop of a hat.

If you find elaborate cooking a challenge, then amuse-bouche could be the answer for you. You can turn the plainest of meals into a gourmet feast by adding a couple to your menu. If, however, you are already an accomplished cook, introducing amuse-bouche to your menu will take your lunch and dinner parties from good to exceptional and you will soon gain a reputation for your wonderful meals.

Whatever your culinary ability, we can all be short on time and so we have coded each recipe with a 'simplicity' level. Some of our amuse-bouches need to be marinated and then cooked before serving, whilst others can be thrown together in minutes. This means that, at a glance, you can judge how long the preparation time will be. The more 'ticks' the recipe is given, the more time you will need to allow. All recipes are for 8 portions, unless otherwise stated.

So let's have fun creating a new experience for our dinner guests. Just like us, once you get hooked, you won't look back...

Amusez les bouches!

Gillie and Dana

amuse-bouche

01. Tureen - Potage de Courge (P22)

02. Egg cup - Oeuf Brouillé (P55)

03. Mini tureen - Vichyssoise (P19)

04. Square dish - Petites Fèves (P31)

05. Tajine - Oeufs de Caille (P54)

06. Presentation plate - Mini-courgette (P33)

07. Mini square dish - Asperges (P68)

08. Skillet - 'Grits' au Fromage (P100)

09. Sauce dish - Crevette d'oeufs de Lump (P81)

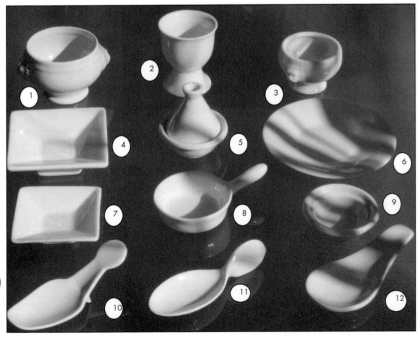

Classic amuse-bouche dishes and spoons - but you can use your own pretty little things; just remember they must be small

presentation dishes

10. Spoon - Anchois Blanc (P59)

11. Spoon - Mangue aux St Jacques (P74)

12. Spoon - Saumon Fumé (P72)

13. Layer verrine - Cocktail de Crevettes (P78)

14. Mini verrine - Crème d'Origan (P35)

15. Mini tankard - Chocolate Pot (P120)

16. Sundae dish - Diplomate au Gingembre (P122)

17. Trou Normand glass - Cerise au Kirsch (P46)

18. Antique verrine - Sucrées en couches (P121)

Classic amuse-bouche verrines - but you can use your own sherry and cocktail glasses and of course, champagne flutes

amuse-bouche

Tom Yum Sauce

Aged Balsamic

Guacamole-style topping

Black Truffle Oil

Teryaki Sauce

Red Onion

Fig

Tamarind Paste

Harissa paste

Sea salt & peppercorns

Lemon

Fennel seeds

Dried chilli 'Pili-pili'

Horseradish powder

Garlic

Tarragon

Star Anise

Onion seeds

Coriander seeds

Paprika

Cardamon

Sweet green pepper

Curry powder

Big flavours for a Lilliputian feast

Hot peppers

Hot red chilli pepper

Potages
Soups

Beetroot
Potage Epicé de Betteraves
Spicy Beetroot Soup with Yoghurt Cubes & Ruby Red Crisps

14

Cucumber
Soupe de Concombre, Courgette et Menthe
Chilled Cucumber, Courgette and Mint soup

15

Carrot
Soupe de Carottes au Cumin et St Jacques
Carrot Cumin Soup with Scallop

16

Lentil
Crème de Lentilles
Lentil Cream

17

Pea
Soupe de Pois Cassés Garnie
Split Pea Soup with Garnishes

18

Potato
Vichyssoise au Basilic
A Chilled Potato and Leek Soup with Basil

19

Scallop
Soupe de Coquille Saint-Jacques à la Crème
Cream of Scallop Soup

20

Tomato
Gaspacho Garni de Céleri
Gaspacho with a Celery Garnish

21

Squash
Potage de Courge avec Biscuits Saumon et Fromage
Butternut Squash Soup with tiny Salmon & Cheese Biscuits

22

Potage Épicé de Betteraves

Spicy Beetroot Soup with Yoghurt Cubes & Ruby Red Crisps

Presentation:
Amuse-bouche verrines or tiny soup bowls

Ingredients
1 large, fresh cooked beetroot, peeled and chopped
1 dessertspoon of olive oil
2 spring onions, chopped
1 tablespoon of freshly grated ginger
1 clove of garlic
1 small hot red chilli, seeds removed and chopped
250 ml/½ pint vegetable stock
Small handful of lemon balm
Small handful of coriander leaves
200 ml/6oz can or carton of coconut milk
1 tablespoon Thai fish sauce
Juice of a lime or a tablespoon of juice from a squeezy bottle
Chopped chives or cream to serve

The colour of this soup is so dramatic and the flavour equally spectacular. Every time we serve it, our guests always try to guess what's in it - and we let them; it all adds to the fun! Serve chilled in little verrines with a scattering of chopped chives or piping hot in tiny bowls with a blob of cream. If you opt for the chilled version, try serving it with the frozen yogurt cubes - delicious. Either way, add a few beetroot crisps (chips) on the side and you cannot fail to impress! You can prepare the soup the day before; indeed, this is important if you are serving it cold.

Method:
Gently fry the onions, garlic, ginger and chilli in the oil for 5 minutes until soft, but not brown. Tear in the lemon balm and coriander and add the stock. Cover and simmer gently for 15 minutes.
Remove from the heat, whiz in the blender and then press the mixture through a sieve into a bowl. Discard the bits in the sieve.
Add the chopped beetroot to the soup and whiz it in a blender until smooth.
Return it to the heat and add the coconut milk, fish sauce and lime juice.
Re-heat gently and serve with a blob of cream or allow to chill overnight and serve with chopped chives.

For the yoghurt garnish:
Mix a small carton of creamy yoghurt with a few teaspoons of chopped chives and freeze in an ice-cube tray at least a day ahead of your meal. Pop a yoghurt cube in each bowl just before serving and snip a few chives over to garnish.

For the beetroot crisps:
Cut wafer thin slices of beetroot and on some parchment paper, bake in a cool oven (150 degrees C) for at least an hour and a half, or until crisp. Allow to completely cool and dry out before serving with the soup.

Soupe de Concombre et Menthe

Chilled Cucumber and Mint Soup

This no-cook chilled soup has a very delicate colour but it is surprisingly full of flavour. It takes minutes to prepare and is a perfect amuse-bouche for a summer's day. You can make it several hours before, cover the bowl with clingfilm/plastic wrap and leave it in the fridge before serving.

Presentation:
Amuse-bouche verrines

Ingredients:
Small tub of natural yoghurt
1 medium sized cucumber
Tablespoon of crème fraiche
Clove of garlic, crushed
Teaspoon of fresh lemon juice
Teaspoon of chopped mint
2 slices of lemon to garnish
2 slices of cucumber to garnish
Salt and pepper

Method:
Peel the cucumber, reserving a few thin slices for the garnish, and retaining a little of the green skin. Slice.
Put the sliced cucumber, garlic, yoghurt and crème fraiche into a blender and whiz until smooth. Add the lemon juice and season with salt and pepper to taste.
Whiz again and then tip into a bowl and add the chopped mint. Chill until ready to serve and then tip into chilled verrines and garnish with tiny slices of cucumber and lemon.

Soupe de Carottes au Cumin et St. Jacques
Carrot Cumin Soup with Scallop

Presentation:
Amuse-bouche bowl and spoon

Ingredients:
1 medium onion, chopped
2tbs/30ml butter
2-3 large carrots - sliced thin
1½ cups/360ml
chicken broth
½ tsp/3ml ground cumin
½ cup/120ml cream
Salt and white pepper
8 scallops - bay size or larger
cut to size
Chives or coriander leaves,
chopped for garnish

The soup can be made a couple days ahead or frozen. Freezing in ice trays and transferring to a freezer bag allows you to take out the portions you need and always have a quick amuse-bouche handy.

Method:
In a saucepan, cook the onion in the butter over moderate heat until softened. Peel and shred the carrots in a food processor or dice by hand and put them in a saucepan. Add the broth, cumin, salt and pepper and simmer the mixture covered until the carrots are very soft. Allow to cool a little and purée in a food processor - if there is any roughness, put the soup through a food mill. Before serving, reheat with the cream.
At serving time lightly sauté a scallop for each person. Pour the soup into the bowls or spoons and top with a scallop. Sprinkle with chives or coriander and serve.

Crème de Lentilles

Lentil Cream

Dry lentils can be cooked to your liking or as a shortcut, a can of drained lentils can be prepared ahead of time and frozen until ready to use. The mixture should be the consistency of a thick purée. When serving, top with crème fraiche or with a thin drizzle of cream, parsley and a bread round.

Presentation:
Amuse-bouche spoon or small cup

Ingredients:
8oz can/240ml prepared lentils
½ cup/120ml chicken broth
½ onion chopped
Salt and pepper
Pinch thyme
Foie gras morsel
Parsley chopped for garnish (optional)

Method:
If cooking dried lentils, cook them according to the package directions with herbs and seasonings above. Drain the cooking liquid and add the chicken broth. If using prepared lentils, simmer the onion in the chicken broth until tender. Then drain the lentils and add to the broth along with the seasonings. Rub the lentil mixture through a sieve or a food mill. The creamed lentils can be frozen at this time. When ready to serve, heat the lentil cream. If too thick, add a little chicken broth. If using raw foie gras, sauté a cube for each dish. If using a prepared foie gras, cut a cube for each person. Place a cube in the bottom of each dish and fill with the warmed lentil cream. Top with a dot of crème fraiche or sour cream. A little parsley will add to the eye appeal.

Soupe de Pois Cassés Garnie

Split Pea Soup with Garnishes

Presentation:
Amuse-bouche soup bowl

Ingredients:
Garnishes: sherry, cream, sour cream or crème fraiche, diced chives, bacon crumble, fried shredded crepes

Soup:
1 cup/47cl dried split peas
1 inch cube salt pork
5 cups/113cl chicken broth
1/2 cup/6cl each diced carrots & onions
1/2 tsp/1/4cl sugar
1tblsp/1cl each of butter and flour mixed together for thickening
Dash of cayenne
Clove of garlic
1 bay leaf
Pinch of thyme

If you do not want to make your own Split Pea Soup, you can use one of the pre-made canned varieties and add some of your own touches. Chilling and reheating the soup intensifies the flavor. The garnishes can be mixed and matched but the sherry has a real infinity for Pea Soup.

Method:
Cook the peas and pork in broth for 2½ hours. Add the rest of the ingredients and cook for half an hour. Serve in bowls and float some sherry on top of the soup and add other garnishes that appeal to you.

Vichyssoise au Basilic

A Chilled Potato and Leek Soup with Basil

This must be served very cold. Make it the day before and leave it in the fridge overnight. The peppery, green basil makes this a very special Vichyssoise and is perfect served as a summer amuse-bouche. For a change, omit the basil from the recipe and serve topped with a piece of smoked salmon, or garnished with chopped cucumber, grated cheese, or a sprig of watercress.

Method:
Melt the butter in a saucepan and add the chopped leeks, onion, potatoes and half the basil leaves. Stir them around in the butter to give them a good coating and sprinkle with salt. Cover and let the vegetables sweat over a very gentle heat for about 20 minutes, giving them a stir from time to time to prevent sticking or browning.
Next add the hot stock and bring to simmering point. Cover and simmer very gently for about 10-15 minutes until the vegetables are soft. Remove from the heat and allow to cool a little before whizzing the mixture in the blender. Pour into a jug and chill. When the soup is cold, add the cream and stir well. Cover with cling-film/plastic wrap and chill overnight.
The next morning bruise the rest of the basil with a pestle to release the oil in the leaves, add to the soup and whiz the mixture in the blender. Chill. When you are ready to serve, divide the soup between your chilled amuse-bouche bowls and garnish with a swirl of cream and a basil sprig.

Presentation:
Amuse-bouche mini soup bowls

Ingredients
Large handful of basil leaves
A few basil sprigs to garnish
70ml/3fl oz thick cream and a little for the garnish
25g/1oz butter
40ml/1½ fl oz vegetable stock
The green leaves of a large leek (trim away the leathery bits), chopped
1 small onion, peeled and chopped
1 large potato, peeled and chopped into cubes
Salt & pepper

Soupe de Coquilles Saint-Jacques à la Crème

Cream of Scallop Soup

This has such a delicate flavour, your guests will beg for more! Serve it after your starter and before the main course. You can prepare the soup and the scallops the day before but don't add the cream and egg yolk until you re-heat the soup before serving.

Presentation:
Tiny soup terrines

Ingredients:
200g/7oz scallops, fresh or frozen (in which case, defrost before cooking)
25g/1oz butter
1 small onion, chopped
225g/8oz peeled potatoes, diced
275ml/½ pint hot fish stock
140ml/¼ pint cold milk
1 large egg yolk beaten together with 40ml/2 fl oz double (thick) cream
A little white wine (optional)
Fresh parsley, chopped
Salt & pepper

Method:
Melt the butter and cook the onions very gently without colouring for about 10 minutes.
Add the diced potatoes and season well. Mix and cover.
Continue to cook very gently for a further 10 minutes and then add the fish stock.
Stir, and cook for a further 10 minutes.
Meanwhile, lightly season 8 scallops and fry them over a high heat in a knob of butter for 30 seconds each side (they should take on a little colour).
Remove from the pan quickly and put each one into a terrine.
Store in the fridge until you are ready to serve.
Remove the roe from the rest of the scallops and retain.
Roughly dice the white flesh.

Put in a pan with the milk and simmer for about 3 minutes.
When the vegetables are cooked, allow to cool and then whiz the mixture through your blender until smooth.
Add the diced scallops, the milk they were cooked in and the roe and stir.
If you think the soup is too thick, then thin it with a little white wine.
Gently re-heat the soup, and just before serving add the egg yolk mixture - but do not boil or else it will curdle.
Pour over the fried scallops and garnish with a little chopped parsley.
Serve straight away.

Gaspacho Garni de Celeri

Gaspacho with Celery Garnish

Take advantage of really nice tomatoes that are available in the summer, otherwise purchase a good pulp/chopped tomato in a box or tin. Garnish this cold soup with a celery stick. Other toppings might be sour cream, or garlic croutons. The gazpacho must be really cold so you can prepare this amuse-bouche well in advance and add the vegetables for garnish just before serving.

Presentation:
Amuse-bouche bowl or glass

Ingredients:
1lb/500g of tomatoes
1 cucumber - preferably seedless
1 red pepper
1-2 green onions
Juice of a lemon plus squeezes of lime to taste
4 teaspoons of olive oil
Several shakes of Tabasco or hot sauce
Salt and pepper
Celery sticks - cut to depth long enough to extend above your dish

Method:
If you are using fresh tomatoes, wash and plunge them into boiling water for 30 seconds. Refresh in cold water and slip off the skins. Remove seeds and cut the flesh into little pieces.
If using prepared tomato pulp, drain liquid and add later if needed.
Peel, cut and small-dice the cucumber, and mince the red pepper.
Put the tomato and half the diced cucumber in a processor. Add oil, lemon and Tabasco. Pulse into a thick soup and correct the seasoning.
Put the soup in serving dishes and chill for at least 1 hour. At serving time, top with minced cucumber and red pepper, sour cream and a celery stick.

Potage de Courge avec

Butternut Squash Soup with Tiny

Presentation:
Baby amuse-bouche tureens
Presentation amuse-bouche plates

Ingredients:
Small butternut squash, peeled, de-seeded and chopped into small chunks
25g /1 oz butter
1 onion, chopped
150m/¼ pt of whole milk
300ml/½ pt vegetable stock
Yesterday's bread
Chilli powder
Salt and pepper

For the cheese biscuits (makes about 14 -16):
1 large slice of smoked salmon
1 egg beaten
100g/4 oz plain flour
1 level teaspoon of English mustard powder
1 level teaspoon of salt
50g/2oz butter chopped
50g/2oz grated cheese
Large pinch cayenne
Sesame seeds/onion seeds

The vibrant colour of the butternut squash soup contrasts both in flavour and crunch with the spicy croutons. Serve it after a simple salad and before a dish of spaghetti and your meal will be transformed. The soup and the croutons can be prepared the day

Method:
Soften the onion in most of the butter, retaining a little for the croutons. Add the chopped squash. Stir and season with salt and pepper. Pop a lid on your pan and simmer very gently for about 10 minutes. Add the milk and the stock and continue to cook, partially covered on a very low heat, for about 15 minutes or until the squash is soft. Cool a little and then blend in a food processor. Chill overnight if preparing the day ahead.

Pre-heat the oven to 200 degrees C. Cut the bread into tiny cubes (allow 3 or 4 per person) and season them with salt, pepper and a sprinkling of chilli powder. Melt a teaspoon of butter or oil in the microwave on an oven-proof plate. Toss the bread cubes in the butter and pop them onto a high shelf in your oven. Cook for about 5 minutes until crisp and golden brown (take care, they can burn very easily!). Re-heat the soup in the microwave until piping hot and carefully fill each little tureen, leaving space for the croutons. Drop a few croutons onto the surface of each and serve immediately.

To make the biscuits:
Preheat the oven to 200 degrees C.
Mix the flour with the mustard powder and salt in a bowl
Rub in the butter with your fingertips until the

Biscuits au Saumon et Fromage

Salmon and Cheese Biscuits

before. The little cheese and salmon biscuits work perfectly with the soup and can also be made the day before. Store both the biscuits and the croutons in an air-tight tin overnight.

mixture resembles bread-crumbs.

Add the grated cheese and the cayenne. Add a dessertspoon of cold water and about half the beaten egg. Mix with a knife and then form a soft dough. Roll out the pastry on a floured surface and use a pastry cutter or the rim of a small glass to cut out the biscuits. Place them on a baking tray lined with baking parchment. With a pastry brush, paint the surface of each biscuit with the remainder of the beaten egg. Sprinkle the lower part of half of the biscuits with onion seeds and the other half with sesame seeds. Cut the smoked salmon into equal pieces and fold each piece onto the top part of each biscuit. Place in the oven and cook for 10-12 minutes until pale golden brown. Remove from the oven and allow to cool on a wire rack.

Coquilles Saint-Jacques Chinoises (page 73)

amuse-bouche

Legumes
Vegetables & Vegetarian Recipes

Artichoke

Artichaut Sauté à la Sauce Rouge   27
Sautéed Artichoke with Red Sauce

Quart d'Artichaut au Four   28
Baked Artichoke Quarter

Asparagus
Asperges Sauce Parmesan   29
Asparagus with Parmesan Sauce

Aubergine/Eggplant   30
Medaillon d'Aubergines au Chèvre
Egg Plant Slices with Goats Cheese

Beans
Petites Fèves au Vin Blancs   31
Baby Broadbeans in a White Wine Sauce

Purée de Haricots Blanc   32
White Bean Purée

Courgette/Zucchini
Mini-Courgette au Parmesan   33
Baby Zucchini with a Parmesan Crust

Endive/Chicory/Radish
Endive Crue Farcie et/ou Sandwich au Radis   34
Stuffed Fresh Endive and/or Radish Sandwich

Oregano/Advacado
Crème d'Origan au Guacamole   35
Oregano Cream with Guacamole

Pepper

Terrine de Poivrons Rouges avec Feta et Pesto   36
Red Pepper Terrine with Feta and Pesto

Sushi

Sushi Balle de Riz et Wasabi Concombre/Cuillère de Sushi   38
Sushi Rice Balls with Wasabi Cucumber/Sushi Spoon

Tomato

Tortellini au Basilic avec Tomates Séchées au Soleil   40
Tortellini with Basil and Sun-dried Tomatoes

Gelée de Tomates avec Mozzarella et Pesto   41
Tomato Jelly with Mozarella and Pesto

Yam/Sweet Potato

Purée de Patates Douces au Gingembre   42
Yam Purée with Ginger

Artichaut Sauté à la Sauce Rouge

Sautéed Artichoke with Red Sauce

Begin with homemade or store bought tomato sauce. The addition of red peppers and Italian sausage or an herb-sage sausage make the sauce a unique contrast to the sautéed artichoke and can be prepared well in advance.

Presentation:
Amuse-bouche plate

Ingredients:
8 artichoke halves - canned or jarred
8oz/225g tomato sauce
8oz/225g jarred red peppers - chopped
6oz/175g flavorful ground sausage
Splash of red wine (optional)
1 tbsp olive oil
Parsley or chives - minced
Butter for cooking

Method:
Prepare the sauce by lightly browning the sausage in a pan with olive oil and adding the chopped red peppers, tomato sauce and a little red wine. Correct the seasoning. The sauce can be prepared days ahead.

At serving time, sautée the cut side of the artichoke heart in a little butter, heat the sauce and place some on each serving dish. Put the artichoke on top of the sauce, cut side up.
Sprinkle with a little minced parsley or chives for garnish.

Quart d'Artichaut au Four

Baked Artichoke Quarter

Presentation:
Amuse-bouche ovenproof casserole

Ingredients:
1cup/240ml mayonnaise - preferably Hellman's
1cup/240ml Parmesan cheese, grated
4 canned artichoke hearts - cut in half or if very large cut 2 hearts in quarters

A very easy and tasty hot amuse-bouche. It can be prepared in individual serving dishes and baked, or baked in one casserole and transferred to the amuse-bouche dishes for serving. Be sure to put a quarter or half of an artichoke in each serving dish. A mayonnaise which does not have mustard, such as Hellman's, works best.

Method:
Preheat oven to 400F/200C
Mix the mayonnaise and Parmesan cheese together. Cut the artichoke hearts and place in each dish. Put the Parmesan mixture on top and bake until golden brown and bubbly.

1.   You can either combine all the ingredients, transfer them to a baking dish and bake until bubbly, then serve in individual dishes.
2.   or place the artichoke hearts in the individual dishes and bake until bubbly.

Serve with bread, a cracker or plain Melba rounds.

Asperges Sauce Parmesan

Asparagus with Parmesan Sauce

This recipe is best served hot but it also works at room temperature. You could also prepare the amuse-bouche ahead of time and briefly run it under the broiler/grill. The delicious Parmesan sauce perfectly complements the asparagus and is enhanced by the crunch of the ham.

Presentation:
Amuse-bouche plate

Ingredients:
8 asparagus tips
1/2 cup/120ml grated Parmesan
1/4 cup/60g butter
1 cup/240ml cream
Salt & pepper if desired
Sautéed shredded ham for garnish - preferably a stronger flavored ham like Black Forest, Parma or Proscuitto

Method:

Sauce:

Put about 1tblsp/30g of butter in a saucepan. Add the cream and simmer for a few minutes to thicken. Then add the grated Parmesan and simmer until dissolved. You may add more cream and Parmesan to adjust the flavor and thickness. Sauce can be made ahead and gently reheated.

Thin slice or chop the ham and sauté in 1tblsp/30g of butter till a little crisp.

Cook asparagus tips in hot sugared water. Blanch them in cold water to keep their color. Dry and place one tip on each plate. Spoon the sauce onto the asparagus.

Sprinkle the ham crisps on top of sauce. Serve immediately or if you have prepared it earlier, run it under the broiler/grill briefly.

Medaillon d'Aubergines au Chèvre

Eggplant Slices with Goats Cheese

Presentation:
Amuse-bouche dish

Ingredients:
1 small eggplant/aubergine about 2 inch/5cm diameter - sliced
1 small log of goats cheese - sliced
Olive oil
Pinch of aromatic herbs for each
4 cherry tomatoes for garnish - cut in half

This is an easy, warm amuse-bouche for a rustic meal. Any goats cheese can be used, but a 'log style' one is easy to slice and put on top of the eggplant/aubergine. Top with fresh herbs from your garden or a pinch of Herbes de Provence. This really needs to be prepared and cooked just before serving, although you could prepare the eggplant/aubergine slices beforehand covered with the salt.

Method:
Cut the eggplant/aubergine in 1/4in/5mm rounds
Place the slices on a paper towel covered plate and sprinkle with salt.
Let them sit for 10 minutes to remove any bitterness, then wipe off salt.
Preheat the oven to 400F/200C.
Place the eggplant/aubergine slices on an oven tray that has been covered with baking paper.
Brush the slices with olive oil and brown in the oven.
Add a slice of goats cheese (cut in rounds) onto the top of the eggplant and reheat for 2 minutes or until cheese is melted.
Top with fresh chopped aromatic herbs, a tomato half or wedge and serve.

Petites Fèves au Vin Blanc

Baby Broadbeans in a White Wine Sauce

The French aren't really into broadbeans so whenever I see them in the market I always buy them and serve them in this delicious sauce. They should always be picked when they are very young, especially for this dish. This makes a delicious vegetarian amuse-bouche that would please veggies as well as the carnivorous. Serve with a little spoon and crusty baguette to soak up the sauce. You could prepare the sauce in advance but do not add the beans until the end or else they will discolour.

Presentation:
Amuse-bouche dishes that will contain a sauce

Ingredients:
Large handful of baby broadbeans, podded (or use lima beans)
1 shallot
Knob of butter
Zest and juice of half a small lemon
50 ml/2 fl oz thick cream
25 ml/1 fl oz white wine
Small handful of chopped mint and parsley
Salt & pepper

Method:
Sauté the shallot in the butter until soft.
Add the white wine, lemon juice and zest and simmer for a few minutes.
Add the thick cream, chopped mint and parsley and re-heat. Do not allow to boil.
Boil the broadbeans for two minutes only, drain and rinse in cold water and then add them to the sauce. Re-heat to simmering point. Season well with salt and pepper.
Divide the mixture between your amuse-bouche dishes, garnish with a sprig of parsley and serve.

Note: I am told that broadbeans are hard to find in the US, too. Why not grow your own? They are a really easy-to-grow vegetable which can be planted straight into the ground in the Autumn or early Spring for an early Summer crop. They freeze well, too.

Purée de Haricots Blancs

White Bean Purée

A bit of "comfort food" on a cold winter night. The velvety texture of the beans topped with the spicy chorizo leaves one wanting more. A little fresh chopped tomato, onion and cilantro/coriander leaf can be added also. The bean mixture can be made days ahead and reheated.

Presentation:
Amuse-bouche soup dish or egg cup

Ingredients:
16oz/454g can of white beans
2tblsp/30ml butter
1 onion chopped
2 cloves garlic pressed or chopped
Salt and white pepper
Herbs such as sage or thyme
1/2-1cup/120-240 ml chicken bouillon
1cup/240ml cream
Chorizo - fine chop approx. 8 tsps for garnish

Method:
Melt the butter in a sauce pan. Add the onion, garlic and a pinch of herbs and sweat them till tender.
Add the drained beans and mix (optional: reserve 8 whole beans for garnish)
Put the bean mixture in a food processing bowl and purée.
Add enough cream for the desired consistency. The purée can now be chilled until ready to serve.
Fine chop enough chorizo to top each soup dish and sauté. Drain on paper towel before adding to the bean mixture. Transfer to a sauce pan to reheat and correct the seasoning with salt and pepper.

Mini-courgettes au Parmesan

Baby Zucchini with a Parmesan Crust

If you grow your own zucchini, then harvest them when they are tiny and you have a delicious amuse-bouche to satisfy your veggie friends, as well as your other guests. You will also find baby zucchini in better supermarkets and grocery stores. They are at their very best when they are no more than 8cm long and served with this delicious Parmesan crust, they are a vegetable to die for. We present them with sorrel leaves which have a zangy fresh taste that complements the cheese perfectly, but any attractive, edible leaf will do. You can prepare them several hours before and then just pop them in the oven before you want to serve them, perhaps after your starter and before your main course.

Presentation:
Amuse-bouche presentation plates

Ingredients
8 baby zucchinis
2 tablespoons of fresh breadcrumbs
2 tablespoons of freshly grated Parmesan
Salt and pepper
Good shake of cayenne pepper
Olive oil
8 sorrel leaves or similar

Method:
Pre-heat the oven to 200 degrees C/400F.
Mix together the breadcrumbs and the grated cheese in a small bowl and season with salt, pepper and cayenne.
Cut the zucchini lengthwise in half and place them on a flat, ovenproof dish. With your fingers, press as much of the breadcrumb mixture on top of each half as you can. Drizzle each one with a little olive oil and bake in the oven for about 5 minutes, until the crumbs are golden brown. Place a sorrel leaf on each presentation plate and arrange two halves on each. Serve straight away - your guests can just pop them in their mouths with their fingers.

Tip: If you can't get baby zucchini and you have a glut of larger ones in your garden, then slice them into rounds and follow the recipe in the same way.

Endive Crue Farcie ou Sandwich au Radis

Stuffed Fresh Endive/Chicory Tip or Radish Sandwich

Presentation:
Amuse-bouche plate

Ingredients for stuffed endive leaves:
8-16 Belgium endive leaves
8-16 spoons of your choice of stuffing
4 cocktail tomatoes cut in half for garnish

The green ends of Belgian endive leaves make good containers for many flavor treats. A few ideas are listed below and many others can be found at the grocery store and then assembled for a quick and easy amuse-bouche. The radish sandwich can be added or served separately. Both can be made ahead, covered and chilled.

Method for stuffed endive leaves:
Cut the endive leaves to desired length and place one or two on each serving plate. Fill with your choice of stuffing. Try with one of the following:
Herbed creamy cheese
Taramasalata
Tapenade
Roquefort & walnut
Caviar & onion sour cream
Mousse Saumon Fumée - see recipe on page 70

Saumon Fumée sur Concombre Crème on page 72
Ceviche

Ingredients and method for radish sandwich:
8 radishes - sliced as a fan
8 buttered bread rounds - cocktail bread or use a cookie cutter
Top with coarse salt, fresh ground pepper and chopped chives

Crème d'Origan au Guacamole

Oregano Cream with Guacamole

In the UK (and possibly in the US?), you can buy a guacamole style topping in a squeezy bottle by a company called Discovery which makes this a quick, easy to prepare amuse-bouche. If you have trouble in finding this or a similar product, you can make your own which is very simple and probably better (recipe below). We always freeze any surplus soup we have made for amuse-bouches so on the base of these verrines, we have used our Potage d'Asperge Verte recipe on page 68 - but you can use any nice, green soup you have. The verrines can be prepared beforehand, clingfilmed/plastic wrapped and left in the fridge for several hours before serving

Presentation:
Amuse-bouche verrines

Ingredients:
Bottle of 'Discovery' guacamole topping (or make your own - see below)
Small amount of green soup
Small handful of baby French beans (runner beans)
8 large cooked and peeled prawns/shrimp (optional - frozen is fine, but defrost beforehand)
Small tub of crème fraiche
Handful of oregano, finely chopped
Small jar of lumpfish caviar (optional)
Salt & pepper

Method:
Chop the beans into tiny pieces and blanch in boiling, salted water for 2 minutes. Drain and combine with the cold soup. Put a teaspoon or two of the mixture in the bottom of each verrine. The beans should just be covered by the soup.

Place a prawn/shrimp on top of the soup so that its bendy back is visible from the side of the glass. If you would prefer this to be a veggie amuse-bouche, then it'll be fine without the prawn/shrimp.

Mix the crème fraiche with the chopped oregano and season lightly. Pile a couple of teaspoons of the mixture on top of the prawn/shrimp.

Squeeze a layer of Discovery guacamole sauce (or put a layer of your home-made version) over this and finally top with a small blob of caviar (again, optional).

Garnish with a tiny sprig of oregano (see if you can find sprigs with little lilac flowers) and serve chilled.

Guacamole:
Cut a ripe avocado in half, remove the pip and scrape the flesh into your blender, along with half a teaspoon of salt and the juice of a lime. Add a small clove of chopped garlic, half a small red onion, a small bunch of coriander and half a fresh red chilli, seeds removed. Whiz until smooth. If you're not going to use it straight away, clingfilm/plastic wrap and refrigerate. Do not make it too far in advance; it discolours. Some people believe that if you leave the pip/pit in the mixture, it helps to retain its colour. It's worth a try!

Terrine de Poivrons Rouges
Red Pepper Terrine

This terrine is quite easy, especially if you use prepared red peppers and is best made a day ahead. You will need a mold that is narrow enough so that a slice will fit on your amuse-bouche

Presentation:
Amuse-bouche plate

Ingredients:
Terrine: Jar of prepared red peppers - cooked, skinned, seeded or pepperdos - the miniature red pepper to be stuffed whole
10oz/300g feta or cream cheese
4 gelatine sheets
1 1/2oz/5 cl liquid cream
Garlic - 1 or more cloves pressed

Method:
Soak the gelatin sheets in a bowl of cold water. When soft, squeeze out the water by hand and heat the gelatin with cream in a saucepan until melted. Put the cheese in a bowl, add cream, garlic and beat with electric mixer until spreadable.
Line a small loaf tin with plastic wrap/cling film (enough to cover the top after assembled). Cut red pepper in strips to fit bottom. Put the strips in the tin and season with salt and pepper. Add a layer of cheese. Then repeat

avec Feta et Pesto
with Feta & Pesto

dish. You can also roll it into a pinwheel and slice. The pesto recipe can be used in other dishes and can be made ahead and chilled or frozen.

Ingredients for the Pesto:
1½cup/375ml basil leaves
2-3 cloves of garlic cut in half
2/3cup/170ml olive oil
½cup/125ml grated Parmesan
½cup/125ml pine nuts
Coarse salt to taste

so that you have 3 layers with the red pepper on top. Chill overnight. When ready to serve, unmold, slice, and decorate with pesto.

Pesto:
Chop basil leaves and garlic in a processor, then dribble in oil through the feed tube while the processor is running. Add pine nuts, Parmesan and salt. Pulse until blended.

Sushi et Concombre au
Sushi Rice Balls with Wasabi

Sushi lends itself perfectly to amuse-bouche and the French are fascinated by these little works of art. They are fiddly, but here are a few that aren't too difficult to assemble and offer an explosion of taste. They can the prepared in advance and kept, covered, in the fridge.

Presentation:
Amuse-bouche presentation plates
Amuse-bouche spoons

Ingredients for the rice balls:
85g/3½oz short-grained rice
100ml/4fl oz water
60g/2½oz rice vinegar
5 dessertspoons caster sugar
Sorrel leaves
Cucumber
Wasabi paste
Smoked salmon (optional)
Gari to garnish (see store cupboard, page 135)

Method (Sushi balls):
To make the Sushi rice, rinse the rice thoroughly until the water runs clear. Drain and put in a pan with the water. Cover, bring to the boil and simmer very gently until all the water is absorbed. Add a little more if the rice isn't completely cooked and allow that to absorb.
Remove from the heat and leave the lid on the pan while you dissolve the sugar in the vinegar over a gentle heat. Allow to cool.
Spread the rice out on a flat dish and drizzle the vinegar

Wasabi et Cuillère de Sushi
Cucumber and Sushi Spoon

Here is another Sushi dish - very easy to prepare once you have made the sushi rice, which will keep in the fridge for a day or two. You can prepare the spoons beforehand, put them on a platter, cover loosely with clingfilm/plastic wrap and refrigerate. It's not really a vegetarian dish (unless your veggies eat fish) but we have included it in this section so that it is with our other Sushi amuse-bouches.

Presentation:
Amuse-bouche spoons

Ingredients for Sushi Spoon:
Sushi rice (see opposite)
Smoked salmon
Lumpfish caviar
Soya sauce
Gari to garnish (see store cupboard page 135)

mixture over the rice. Toss gently with a wooden spoon, while fanning (use your hairdryer on a cool setting!). Cover the rice with a damp tea towel until you are ready to use it.

Using a melon baller, scoop out little balls of cucumber for each amuse bouche.

Put a small square of clingfilm/plastic wrap onto your work surface and crisscross two sorrel leaves. Put a small amount of Sushi rice on top of the leaves and then a tiny bead of wasabi paste in the centre. Top with a cucumber ball and some more rice.

Fold the leaves around the mixture as tightly as possible to form a ball and then wrap the clingfilm around that. Twist the ends to make a tight ball. Refrigerate until you are ready to serve.

For a change, substitute a small slice of smoked salmon for the sorrel leaves, omit the wasabi paste from the centre of the Sushi and garnish with a small drop instead.

Serve either on an amuse-bouche plate or spoon with a few drops of soya sauce and a few threads of Gari (see store cupboard recipe, page 135).

Method (Sushi spoons):
Cut out pieces of smoked salmon to neatly fit your amuse-bouche spoon.
Heap a small amount of Sushi rice on top.
Finish with a small teaspoon of caviar as shown.
Serve with a few drops of soya sauce and garnish with threads of Gari (see store cupboard recipe, page 135).

Tortellini au Basilic et Tomates Séchées au Soleil

Tortellini with Basil and Sun-dried Tomatoes

Presentation:
Amuse-bouche plates
Cocktail sticks

Ingredients:
8 fresh spinach and ricotta tortellini
4 sun-dried tomatoes, halved
8 large basil leaves
Small teaspoon of grated lemon zest
2 dessertspoons lemon juice
4 dessertspoons olive oil
Salt & pepper

Store Cupboard:
Jar of sun-dried tomatoes (140)

The tortellini is marinated in lemon before being skewered together with basil-wrapped sun-dried tomatoes. We used our own 'sun-dried' tomatoes (see store cupboard recipe page 140) but you can buy them in jars from any good grocery store. You can make the marinade the day before and the tortellini can be soaking up the lemon flavours overnight. Prepare the little skewers up to four hours before the meal; they will do fine in the fridge. Remember to take them out at least an hour before you serve them; they should be at room temperature.

Method:
Cook the tortellini in a large volume of boiling water for about 4 minutes - or according to the instructions of the packet. Drain and rinse in cold water. Allow to cool on a piece of paper towel. Put the oil, lemon juice, zest, salt and pepper into a screw-topped jar and shake well. When the tortellini is cool, tip into a bowl and carefully combine with the marinade. Allow to marinate at room temperature for at least half an hour.

To assemble, pour a little of the marinade onto each amuse-bouche plate. Half wrap each piece of tomato with a basil leaf. Spear a tortellini with a cocktail stick and then thread on the tomato with its basil leaf. Place it on top of the marinade and garnish as desired.

Gelée de Tomates avec Mozzarella et Pesto

Tomato Jelly with Mozzarella and Pesto

When the garden (or the supermarket!) is full of sweet cherry tomatoes, make this amuse-bouche which combines three flavours that were made for each other in heaven: tomato, basil and mozzarella. Serve them at the start of your meal or even as a Trou Normand (without the cheese) before the main course. You will probably end up with too much pesto, but keep it in the fridge for snacking the next day. The jellies should be made the day before but don't make the pesto too far ahead otherwise it will discolour.

Presentation:
Amuse-bouche verrines or presentation dishes

Ingredients:
Large handful of basil leaves
1 tablespoon pine nuts
3 garlic cloves
25g/1 oz Parmesan cheese, finely grated
6 tablespoons olive oil
75g/ 3oz cherry tomatoes
Thyme sprigs
Extra basil leaves
4 gelatine leaves
Mozzarella ball
Salt & pepper

Method:
Roast the cherry tomatoes in a moderate oven for half an hour with two of the cloves of garlic, the herbs, salt and pepper.

When the tomatoes are cooked, remove the thyme sprigs and whiz them through the blender.

Soak the gelatine leaves in a dish of cold water for 5 minutes.

Press the mixture through a sieve and return to a pan. Thin with a little red or rosé wine if necessary. Reheat (without boiling), squeeze out the gelatine and add it to the warm mixture, stirring until dissolved.

Divide the mixture between the verrines or small, individual jelly moulds, cover with clingfilm/plastic wrap and chill overnight.

To make the pesto, all you have to do is to put the basil leaves, pine nuts, a garlic clove and the oil into the blender and whiz until smooth. Put the pesto in a dish and cover with a little oil to stop it from discolouring.

To serve, dip the moulds into some very hot water so that they can be turned out more easily. Put a thin slice of mozzarella on your little dishes, top with the jelly and garnish with a blob of pesto. If you plan to serve the jelly in the verrines, cut small circles of mozzarella to fit the top of the glasses and top with a blob of pesto.

Purée de Patates Douces au Gingembre

Yam Purée with Ginger

This recipe is tastier and richer if made with the orange colored yam rather than the yellowish sweet potato. The purée can be made a couple days ahead and reheated.

Presentation:
Amuse-bouche spoon or bowl

Ingredients:
1 yam or sweet potato
½ tsp/2.5ml ginger - fresh grated or powdered
1 tsp/5ml of butter
Salt to taste
Cream - start with a ¼ cup/ 60ml and add more as needed
Crème fraiche, minced candied ginger and parsley for garnish

Method:
Peel and cut the yam in cubes and steam them until soft or simmer in a little sugar water.
Grate the fresh ginger with a fine grater to achieve a pastelike consistency.
Put the cooked yam, ginger paste and ¼ cup/60ml cream in a processor and whizz. Add more cream or a little water if necessary to easily purée the potato. Consistency should be moister than a mashed potato but not soupy. Reheat to serve, correct seasoning and top with garnishes

Trou Normand*

Palate Cleansers

Bloody Mary Sorbet *Bloody Mary Sorbet*	44
Boule de Poire au Vin Rouge *Pear Ball in Spiced Red Wine*	45
Cerise au Kirsch *Cherries in Kirsch*	46
Citron Givré *Lemon Ice Cream in a Lemon Shell*	47
Gelée de Cassis *Blackcurrant Jelly*	48
Melon Charentais au Pastis *Melon in Pastis*	49
Sorbet de Fraise *Strawberry Sorbet & other Sorbet Recipes*	50

*Strictly speaking, a Trou Normand is a glass of spirits served between courses to aid digestion. Here we have jazzed the idea up a little to include fruits, sorbets and ice-cream to be more like an American or English palate cleanser

Sorbet au Bloody Mary

Bloody Mary Sorbet

Presentation:
Champagne flutes
Bendy straws

Ingredients:
400 ml/ ¾ pint tomato juice
3 tablespoons vodka
A further tot of vodka for each glass (optional!)
2 dashes of Worcestershire sauce
A dash of Tabasco
1 tablespoon lemon juice
Salt & black pepper
Mint to garnish

This makes a change from the usual sweet mid-course Trou Normand. With a shot of vodka in the bottom of each glass, it will certainly help to get your party going! Serve with a straw and invite your guests to suck the vodka through the sorbet before resorting to a spoon!

Method:
Put all the ingredients into your blender jug and give it a good mix with a stick blender. Pour the mixture into a shallow tray and freeze.

Every hour or so, tip the mixture back into the jug and give it another whiz with the stick blender before returning to the freezer. Repeat 4 or 5 times until you have the right consistency for a sorbet. Then allow to freeze thoroughly. Alternatively, use an ice-cream machine, if you have one.
When you're ready to serve, put a shot of vodka in the base of each flute. Using an ice-cream scoop, put a ball of sorbet into each glass. Garnish with a tomato stalk or with a sprig of mint. Pop a bendy straw in each glass and serve immediately.

Boule de Poire au Vin Rouge

Pear Ball in Spiced Red Wine

This recipe could be a palate cleanser between courses or a pre-dessert amuse-bouche. The spiced wine freezes well and if frozen in ice cube trays, you will have a lot of flexibility as to numbers and uses. Also the pear ball can be simmered then frozen like a sorbet for hot summer days. Another option is to serve it warm in winter, or for a seasonal touch at Christmas.

Method:
Assemble all the ingredients except for the pear in a sauce pan. Simmer until about one third has evaporated. Correct seasoning. Proportions of flavorings will obviously depend upon the amount and type of wine you use and personal taste. Chill or freeze. If you are using frozen cubes of spiced wine, thaw well ahead of serving time.

Make the pear balls. Simmer them in enough spiced wine to cover until they are colored and soft. Drain wine back into your spiced wine. Pear balls can be chilled or frozen to serve as a sorbet.

To serve, place a pear ball in each glass and cover with spiced wine. Invite your guest to drink from the glass or serve with a cocktail stick.

Presentation:
Amuse-bouche liquor glass or egg cup

Ingredients:
1-2 pears made into 8 balls with a melon baller
½ bottle of red wine - it is a good use for saved, leftover wine
Orange peel - couple of strips made with a vegetable peeler
Sugar to taste
1 cinnamon stick
Pinch of fresh grated nutmeg
½ lemon - juiced
3 cloves - optional

Cerise au Kirsch

Cherries in Kirsch

Presentation:
Pretty little liquor glasses

Ingredients:
Cherries from the garden in liquor, or a tin or bottle of store-bought cherries
Liquor of your choice (Cassis or Kirsch are good choices)
Fresh cherries for garnish

To make this little Trou Normand, you need to prepare the cherries well in advance - about two years before, ideally! We pick our cherries from the tree in the garden, prick them with a pin (or de-pip them), pack them into sterilised jars and cover them in a liquor such as brandy, Kirsch or port. They then go into the store cupboard for at least two years.
If you can't wait that long to serve this simple little Trou Normand then use tinned or bottled cherries from your grocery store.

Method:
If you don't have any cherries that you have bottled previously in liquor, then put two store-bought tinned cherries per head into a small bowl and cover with the liquor of your choice at least 24 hours before you intend to serve them. Cover with clingfilm/plastic wrap and chill.
If you're using your own bottled cherries, put two cherries into each glass, fill the glass to the top with the liquor in which they have been soaking. Garnish with a fresh cherry with a stalk and serve between courses.

Citron Givré

Lemon Ice Cream in a Lemon Shell

This is an easy ice cream to make and does not require an ice cream maker. Beat the ingredients with a mixer and freeze. Serve as a palate cleanser or a pre-dessert. Either way, it's deliciously refreshing.

Presentation:
Amuse-bouche glass or bowl to hold lemon half

Ingredients:
Equal portions of 1 cup/240ml each of sugar, milk and cream
Juice of 2 lemons and zest
8 half lemon shells

Method:
Chill the cream and milk.
With an electric mixer, blend the sugar and lemon juice.
Add the milk and cream and beat until well blended.
Add the lemon zest and pour into a freezer box/tray.
When almost frozen but a bit mushy in the center, remove and beat again. This should eliminate the ice crystals and make a smoother ice cream.
Refreeze until ready to eat.
At this point you could also freeze in single portions.
Fill a lemon half or an amuse-bouche dish and garnish with a mint leaf.

Gelée de Cassis

Blackcurrant Jelly

Presentation:
Verrines

Ingredients:
8 tablespoons of Cassis
Cup of fresh or frozen (but defrosted) blackcurrants
2 sheets of gelatine
Mint to garnish

Cassis is often served as an aperitif in France, usually to flavour a local bubbly white wine. The sharpness of the berries and sweetness of the Cassis makes this a superb Trou Normand and is simplicity itself to make. You can make these up a day or two in advance; cover and chill in the fridge.

Method:
Soak the gelatine sheets in a bowl of cold water for 5-10 minutes.
Set a blackcurrant per person aside to garnish. Put the rest in a small pan with the Cassis and bring to the boil. Simmer gently, without stirring, for two minutes. Remove from the heat and add the gelatine, stirring well until completely dissolved. Take care not to crush the berries.
Using a slotted spoon, place equal portions of berries into the verrines.
Top up with the liquid jelly and allow to cool before putting in the fridge for at least 4 hours to set.
To serve, garnish with a tiny sprig of mint and a whole berry per verrine.

Melon Charentais au Pastis

Melon in Pastis

We love the minty flavour of the Pastis with the chilled melon - a really refreshing in-between course Trou Normand. If you prefer something sweeter then substitute the Pastis with a peach liqueur. If you want more kick, add a shot of vodka. Whatever your choice of liqueur, let the melon balls marinate in it for several hours before serving.

Presentation:
Port glass or verrine
Pretty saucer

Ingredients:
1 small Charantais/Canteloupe melon
8 shots of Pastis (or other liqueur)
Fresh mint sprigs to garnish

Method:
Cut the melon in half and discard the seeds. Using a melon baller, scoop out tiny balls of melon and make a little pyramid in each of the verrines. Pour the Pastis over the melon balls and garnish with a sprig of fresh mint. Chill in the fridge for several hours before serving.

amuse-bouche

Sorbet de Fraise

Strawberry Sorbet

Presentation:
Port glass or verrine

Ingredients:
Tub of strawberry sorbet
Teaspoon of Cassis
1 strawberry per person
Basil leaves
Freshly ground black pepper

You can buy delicious sorbets in all sorts of flavours at your local store these days and they make a perfect palate cleanser. Served before the main course, they are intended to facilitate for what comes next. Here we have used strawberry; the basil and a brief grind of black pepper bring out the flavour of the strawberries. To make life a little easier, you could chill your glasses, complete with the liquor of your choice, in the fridge before your guests arrive. Other sorbet and liquor suggestions are listed below.

Method:
Take the sorbet from the freezer and allow to soften a little. Put a teaspoon of Cassis into each verrine and using a wet ice-cream scoop or a teaspoon, form a ball of sorbet and pop it on top of the Cassis. Grind with a little black pepper. Decorate with two strawberry halves and top with tiny basil leaves.

Sorbet suggestions:
Lime or lemon sorbet with tequila
Peach sorbet with Benedictine
Orange sorbet with Drambuie or Cointreau
Apricot sorbet with apricot brandy and dry vermouth
Cherry sorbet with vodka and a dash of Pernod
Coffee ice-cream with Tia Maria or amaretto
Raspberry sorbet with white rum
Passion fruit sorbet with dark rum and a dash of maraschino
Raspberry sorbet with Calvados and a dash of Chartreuse
Blackcurrant sorbet with Cassis
Garnish with a suitable piece of fruit, mint or basil leaves.

Oeufs
Eggs

Quails Eggs

Crème d'Epinards avec Oeuf de Caille   52
Creamed Spinach with Baked Quail Egg

'One-eyed Susan'   53
One-eyed Susan

Oeufs de Cailles à la Crème Fraîche   54
Quails Eggs poached in Sour Cream

Hens Eggs

Oeuf Brouillé aux Anchois et Ciboulette   55
Scrambled Egg with Anchovies and Chives

Quiche Lorraine Classique   56
Classic Quiche Lorraine

Crème d'Epinards avec Oeuf de Caille
Creamed Spinach with Baked Quail Egg

Presentation:
Amuse-bouche ovenproof edged dish

Ingredients:
8oz/250ml spinach - chopped
2tbsp/30ml butter
1cup/240ml cream
Small onion - chopped (optional)
Salt & pepper
Pinch ground nutmeg
8 quail eggs
4tsp/20ml cheese - shredded for topping (optional)
Paprika for garnish

Frozen chopped spinach works well for creaming but fresh is delicious if you have the time. You can prepare the creamed spinach ahead of time and place in your ovenproof serving dishes. At serving time, top with the raw egg and bake the amuse-bouche.

Method:
Preheat oven to 400F/200C. Thaw the frozen chopped spinach and remove the liquid by putting in a strainer and pressing. Cook the onion in the butter. Add the spinach, cream, salt and pepper and a pinch of nutmeg. Add more cream, butter and spices as needed throughout the cooking. When tender and still creamy put the warm mixture in the serving dishes and break a raw quail egg on top. Top with cheese if you like and bake in the oven to cook the egg. Sprinkle with a little paprika and serve.

*Tip - If you have chilled the spinach mixture, bring it to room temperature or pre-heat it in the oven before topping with the egg.

'One-eyed Susan'

One-eyed Susan

Presentation:
Amuse-bouche presentation
plates

Ingredients:
8 quails eggs
8 slices of brioche
Butter for frying
Chopped chives to garnish

This up-market version of egg on toast was the brainchild of the late chef Jean-Louis Paladin. It makes a delightful and funny amuse-bouche and is probably best served at the beginning of the meal. In France, we can get sliced brioche in small, round loaves but if you have to use a whole brioche, then you can cut out the circles earlier in the day and have your frying plan 'ready-to-go' before your guests arrive.

Method:
If you can buy a small, round, sliced brioche loaf, then take one slice per person and using a 2-3cm/1inch cutter, cut out a central circle in each slice. If you are using a brioche loaf, cut slices as thin as you can, and then, using a 6cm/2 inch cutter, cut out circles from each slice of brioche. Using a 2-3cm/1inch cutter, cut out an inner-circle from the larger circles.

Melt enough butter to cover the bottom of the pan and place the hoops of brioche in the butter. Lightly sauté on one side and flip over. Take off the heat if you aren't going to serve straight away; cover the pan with a cloth until you're ready to cook.

Break a quails egg into each middle circle; it's easier to break each one into a small cup beforehand and then tip it into the circle, just in case the yolk breaks and you need to start again. Season lightly. Cook for about a minute over a moderate heat until the whites are set and the yolks are still runny.

Using a slotted spatula, transfer each Susan onto a presentation plate and sprinkle with a little chopped chives. Serve straight away - and watch your guests smile!

Oeufs de Cailles à la Crème Fraiche
Quails Eggs poached in Sour Cream

Presentation:
Amuse-bouche tajines

Ingredients:
8 quails eggs
Small tub of crème fraiche
Butter
Chives, chopped finely
Paprika
Salt & pepper

Served in these little tajines, this amuse-bouche never fails to delight our guests. When they lift the lids, they have no idea what's in store for them! So simple, but a real crowd-pleaser! You can prepare them beforehand and chill until ready to steam.

Method:
Grease each tajine thoroughly with the butter, especially around the top, where the lid meets the bowl.
Put a sprinkling of chopped chives in the bottom of each tajine and then carefully break a quails egg on top.
Season well with salt and pepper and then add a small teaspoon of crème fraiche to cover. Do not overfill. Dust with a little paprika, sprinkle with a few chopped chives and close the lid.

When the steamer is hot, steam the closed tajines for 4-5 minutes, depending on the efficiency of your steamer. Do not overcook, because the yolk should still be runny. Don't forget, the eggs will continue to cook whilst you are getting them to the table.

Note: All steamers vary in efficiency so it's worth having a test run on this recipe

Oeuf Brouillé aux Anchois et Ciboulette

Scrambled Egg with Anchovies and Chives

Simple scrambled eggs jazzed up with anchovy and chives are simply and quickly made in the microwave but you can use a traditional small pan with a little melted butter if you prefer. Either way, do not over-cook: the egg should still be soft and a little runny. This is a perfect amuse-bouche for a house-party 'brunch; cook the eggs whilst your guests sit round the table with a glass of Bucks Fizz/fresh orange with bubbly.

Presentation:
Pretty egg cups
Amuse bouche plates

Ingredients:
4 eggs
8 anchovies
Chopped chives/8 whole ones, halved, to garnish
2 tablespoons of single cream
Black pepper

Method:
Break the eggs into a small bowl. Beat in the cream, chopped chives and black pepper, but no salt. Cut each anchovy in half lengthways and curl 8 halves up to garnish. Finely chop the other halves and add to the mixture. Microwave in 30 second bursts, scramble with a fork and continue to cook until set or cook on the hob/stove in the traditional way. The mixture should still be a little runny. Pile into egg cups, carefully place the curled anchovy on top and arrange the chives to form a cross. Serve immediately.

Quiche Lorraine Classique
Classic Quiche Lorraine

Presentation:
Amuse-bouche plate

Ingredients:
Pack of shortcrust pastry
1 whole egg and 1 egg yolk
140ml/5 fl oz double cream
50g/2oz smoked lardons or a few slices of smoked bacon, chopped into tiny pieces
50g/2oz grated Parmesan Cheese
Salt and pepper

Quiche Lorraine Hawaiian:
1 slice of pineapple, cut into small pieces
Mild chilli powder

No French cookbook would be complete without a Quiche Lorraine - so here is our amuse-bouche version. If you want to jazz it up a bit try our Quiche Lorraine Hawaiian. These are best served straight from the oven when they are still lovely and puffy but they taste good cold, too. You will probably have enough pastry and mixture to make a few extra, which will make a nice snack the next day.

Method:
Pre-heat oven to 180C /350F. Roll out the pastry and using a 6cm/2½ inch pastry cutter or glass rim, cut out 8 circles. Grease a patty/muffin tin with a little butter and line each mould with a pastry circle, carefully pushing the pastry down into the well and up its sides. Prick the base of each quiche a couple of times with a fork.

Fry the chopped bacon over a quick heat in a non-stick pan until crisp and then remove them to a piece of kitchen roll.

Place a couple of the bacon pieces/lardons (break them up if they're too long) in each quiche and then divide the grated cheese between them, pressing the filling down gently.

For the Hawaiian quiches, put a piece of pineapple in each quiche and give each a generous shake of chilli powder before adding the cheese.

In a jug, beat the egg and egg yolk together with the cream and season with plenty of black pepper but only a little salt. Pour a little of the mixture into each quiche, dividing it between them. Don't over-fill.

Bake for 18-20 minutes until the quiches are well-risen and golden brown. Serve straight away if you want them to look their best.

Poissons et Crustaces

Fish & Shellfish

Anchovies
Anchois Blanc sur un Lit Vert   59
White Anchovies on a Bed of Creamed Wasabi

Caviar
Mini-Blini avec Caviar et Oignons   60
Mini blini with Caviar and Onion

Caviar à la Crème de Pomme de Terre   61
Caviar with Potato Cream

Deux Caviars   62
Two Caviar

Crab
Tomate Cerise Farcie de Crabe au Curry   63
Cherry Tomato stuffed with Curried Crab

Mixed fish
Filet de Poisson à la Creme de Fenouil   64
Fish fillet with Fennel Cream

Verrine Nordique à la Crème Citronée   65
Nordic Verrine with Lemon Cream

Mussels
Moules au Curry ou Moules avec Chorizo et Tomates   66
Mussels in Curry Sauce or with Chorizo & Tomato

Oysters
Huitres Crues sur Crème d'Artichauts   67
Raw Oysters on Artichoke Cream

Salmon
Fagots d'Asperges Vertes au Saumon Fumé   68
Asparagus Tips Wrapped in Smoked Salmon/Asparagus Soup

Mousse de Saumon Fumée   70
Mousse of Smoked Salmon

Anchois Blancs sur un Lit Vert

White Anchovies on a bed of Creamed Wasabi

This amuse-bouche has quite a kick! It's very easy to put together and will have your guests taking a deep, satisfied gasp. You can prepare it several hours before serving it at the beginning of your meal.

Presentation:
Amuse-bouche spoons

Ingredients
4 white anchovies
Small tub of crème fraiche (or an equal mixture of Horseradish/crème fraiche for extra 'kick')
Tube of Wasabi paste
Cucumber slices
Black pepper

Method:
Mix 4 teaspoons of crème fraiche with 2 teaspoons of Wasabi paste and season with black pepper. Put a small teaspoon of the mixture into each spoon. Cut the anchovies in half along the spine and then curl up each half to fit the spoon. Cut the cucumber slice into little wedges and garnish.

Mini Blini avec Caviar et Oignons
Mini Bini with Caviar and Onions

Presentation:
Amuse-bouche plate

Ingredients:
Jar of black or red lumpfish caviar
8 mini blinis
1 small onion - chopped
3 cooked quail eggs or a small chopped hard boiled egg
4tsp sour cream or crème fraiche

For those rushed days or after-work dinners, this simple little dish will liven up the plainest of meals. Just assemble for a quick and easy amuse-bouche.

Method:
Warm the blinis, if you like, and then top with the caviar (one color or both).
Decorate with the sour cream, chopped onion and chopped egg.
To add an authentic touch, you could serve this with a thimble of vodka.

Caviar à la Crème de Pommes de Terre
Caviar with Potato Cream

Presentation:
Amuse-bouche bowl or verrine

Ingredients:
2 medium potatoes
Half a small onion
White pepper & salt to taste
Liquid cream - amount depends on type and size of potato
Small jar of black lumpfish caviar
Basil oil or bit of pesto for garnish (optional)

This is a taste delight with the cool potato cream gracing the caviar hidden beneath. A surprise for your guests. The potato cream can be made a couple days ahead and the amuse-bouche assembled at serving time.

Method:
Peel and dice 2 medium potatoes and place in small pan. Add cream to cover. Add pinch of salt and white pepper.
Simmer until very soft as for a mashed potato (add more cream if necessary).
With a garlic press, squeeze the juice from the onion into the pan toward end of the cooking.
When cooked, purée in food processor till smooth (add more cream if needed to get a consistency that is between mashed potato and liquid).
Correct seasoning and chill.
Near serving time, put the caviar in the bottom of a verrine and top with potato cream.
After assembly, it can be held in the fridge for an hour or so.
Garnish top with basil oil dots or some pesto and serve.

Deux Caviars

Two Caviars

Presentation:
Amuse-bouche dish or spoon

Ingredients:
1 jar each of red and black caviar
Small container of crème fraiche/sour cream for garnish on top - optional
Chives or onion (chopped) optional on top
4 cooked, peeled quail eggs, halved - optional
8 toast rounds

This is a quick-and-easy, no-cook amuse-bouche that will add a touch of elegance to your meal, especially if you can buy the pre-cooked and peeled quail eggs at your store. Otherwise, buy the raw ones, boil and peel them yourself. All you have to do is arrange a pattern to fit your dish. Let your imagination create a design. It can be prepared ahead of time and chilled.

Method:
Arrange one or two colors of caviar in your dish/spoon and garnish. If using the quail eggs, cut them in half lengthwise and place on top of the caviar. If you wish, you may garnish with a touch of crème fraiche/sour cream sprinkled with chopped chives or a little onion juice or fine diced onion added to the sour cream. Serve with a toast round.

Tomate Cerise Farcie de Crabe au Curry
Cherry Tomato Stuffed with Curried Crab

Another amuse-bouche that you can easily assemble before serving if you do the prep work ahead of time. It is nice for a summer dinner in the garden.

Presentation:
Amuse-bouche plate or spoon

Ingredients:
6½ oz/175g can of crab
2oz/50g mayonnaise
1 fine chopped green onion
2tsp/10ml mild curry powder or to taste
1tsp/5ml garam masala - optional
Salt and pepper
Pinch of sugar
Pinch cayenne
8 cherry tomatoes
Parsley for garnish

Method:
Ahead of serving, chop the green onion, drain the can of crab and mix all ingredients together, except for the tomato and the parsley. Correct seasoning and chill until ready to use.

At serving time or half an hour ahead, remove the stem end from tomato and remove seeds. Drain the tomatoes on some paper towel. When it's time to serve, make a slight cut across bottom of tomato so it will sit flat and not roll when stuffed.

Stuff with the crab mixture and garnish with parsley.

Filet de Poisson à la Crème de Fenouil
Fish Filet with Fennel Cream

Presentation:
Amuse-bouche plate

Ingredients:
10 -12oz/300g firm white fish
4tblsp flour seasoned with salt and pepper or Cajun spice
Grape seed oil for frying (less absorbent)
Medium fennel bulb
2oz/50g butter for cooking
2cup/450g cream plus extra if it cooks too dry
2tsp/10ml mild curry powder
Salt and white pepper

The sauce takes a little cooking time but can be made ahead and frozen. Using an ice cube tray to freeze small portions of sauce works really well and the cubes can be transferred to a freezer bag for storage. The curry powder is a hidden ingredient. It adds a subtle flavor but should not be of a quantity to taste like a curry. Any firm white fish will do - panga, catfish, perch, pike, etc.

Method:
Sauce: Thinly slice the fennel and sweat in the butter until very soft. Add cream and curry powder to lightly flavor. Add salt and white pepper to taste. Cook the fennel until very soft and creamy, the consistency of gravy. You may have to add cream throughout the cooking.
Cut the fish into 8 servings to fit your amuse-bouche dishes. Dust with seasoned flour. Sauté on medium to high heat till browned and crispy. Place sauce in serving dish and top with fish.
Garnish with a fennel frond.

Verrine Nordique à la Crème Citronée

Nordic Verrine with Lemon Cream

Don't cut back on the lemon juice in this recipe; the saltiness of the fishy bits need the sharpness of the lemon. The finished verrine looks spectacular with its pretty stripes of white, red, black and pink and topped with little white anchovies (don't use the brown salty ones in tins), it is a very tasty amuse-bouche. You can make this up several hours in advance but not the day before because the lumpfish eggs will sink into the lemon cream. We like to serve this at the beginning of the meal, before the first course.

Presentation:
Amuse-bouche verrines

Ingredients
2 slices of smoked salmon
8 cooked, peeled prawns/shrimp
Pot of black lumpfish eggs
Pot of red lumpfish eggs
8 white anchovies
2 teaspoons of chopped fresh basil
2 teaspoons of chopped fresh dill
Juice of 2 lemons
4 tablespoons of thick crème fraiche
Black pepper

Method:
To make the lemon cream, add the lemon juice, basil and dill to the crème fraiche and season with black pepper, but no salt. Gently stir the mixture so that the lemon cream remains firm. Chill for half an hour or so. Put a teaspoon on the lemon cream into the bottom of each verrine. Add a teaspoon of red lumpfish to cover. Now put in another layer of lemon cream and then a layer of black lumpfish. Cut the smoked salmon into small strips and roll each one up. Top each verrine with a roll of smoked salmon and a prawn/shrimp. Cut each anchovy into two down the spine and lay them criss-cross over the top of the verrine. Chill. Garnish with a little dill and serve.

Simplicity level: ✔✔

Moules au Curry ou Moules avec Chorizo et Tomate

Mussels in Curry Sauce or with Chorizo and Tomato

Presentation:
Amuse-bouche mussel shell or rimmed dish

Ingredients:
8 mussels - 1 for each person

Curry Sauce:
8oz/25g cream
1-2tsp/5-10ml curry powder - mild, medium or hot
1tsp/5 ml garam masala - optional
1 small onion-fine chopped
1tblsp/15ml butter
Salt and pepper
Garnish fine chopped parsley or coriander

Chorizo Tomato Sauce:
4 slices chorizo - ½ inch thickness
1cup/25g tomato sauce

The quickest option is to buy frozen cooked and shelled mussels. Unfreeze the number you want for your amuse-bouche and save the rest for another time. You can prepare either of these sauces beforehand and they freeze well. Defrost the mussels in the fridge overnight. Alternatively throw a handful of fresh mussels into a pan of boiling water and steam for about 5 minutes until they open.

Method:
Thaw the mussels if frozen.
Curry Sauce: Sweat onion and butter in saucepan. Then add the cream and curry powder. Simmer till the onion is cooked. Correct seasoning.
Tomato Chorizo Sauce: Sauté the chorizo and drain on a paper towel. Add the chorizo to 1cup/25g of tomato sauce.
The sauces can be chilled until ready to use.
When you are ready to serve, Tip the mussels into the sauce and bring to simmering point before transferring to the serving dishes.
Alternatively, place the mussels and cold sauce in ovenproof dishes and heat through in the oven. Top with a pinch of chopped herbs.

Huitres Crues sur Crème d'Artichaut

Raw Oysters on Artichoke Cream

Presentation:
Amuse-bouche spoon

Ingredients:
8 fresh oysters
8 small artichoke hearts - canned or jarred
1 tbs/15ml lemon juice - optional
Water
Lemon zest to garnish
Chives, chopped to garnish

The use of lemon depends on the artichokes you purchase. Some have a citrus flavor already and some do not. A small or medium oyster usually works best. An optional way of serving this is to use a bowl and place the artichoke paste in the bottom. Chop the oysters and mix some lemon juice and zest with its liquid before putting on top of the artichoke. Sprinkle with chives and serve with a spoon. Either way, you can make the artichoke cream beforehand and add the oyster just before serving.

Method:
Drain and mash the artichoke heart. Add a little water and cook on low till very tender. Drain excess water and reserve.
Place the hearts in a food processor bowl and purée until smooth. Add some reserved water as needed and some lemon juice to your taste. Chill.
When ready to serve, place a dollop of the artichoke cream in the bottom of each spoon. Open oysters and place one on top of each spoon.
Garnish with a good pinch of zest and chives.

Fagots d'Asperges

Asparagus Tips wrapped in

Presentation:
Amuse-bouche plates

Ingredients:
8 blanched asparagus tips
Pinch of bicarbonate of
soda/baking soda
Slice or two of smoked salmon
Lemon cream (see recipe for
Verre Nordique on page 65)
Dill to garnish

These little fagots not only look very impressive, they have a juicy, fresh flavour and can't fail to please. You can prepare them several hours before and chill, but the dill should be arranged

Method:
Snap off the tough ends of the asparagus and discard. Cut off eight 6cm/2½ inch asparagus tips. Blanch the tips in boiling, salted water with a pinch of bicarbonate of soda for 90 seconds (the bicarbonate helps the tips keep their lovely green colour). Drain and cool. Cut small strips of smoked salmon and roll around each blanched asparagus tip. Put a small teaspoon of lemon cream on each amuse-bouche plate and then carefully place the wrapped tip on top of the cream. Garnish with dill and serve chilled.

Vertes au Saumon Fumé

Smoked Salmon/Asparagus Soup

Presentation:
Amuse-bouche tureens

Ingredients:
1 small onion (chopped)
25g/1oz butter
450g/1 lb asparagus
1 tsp plain flour
250ml/½ pint chicken stock
50ml/2 fl oz crème fraiche
Salt & pepper

criss-cross just before you serve, otherwise they will wilt. Use the rest of the asparagus spears to make the soup below, which will freeze beautifully for another occasion.

For the soup:
Simplicity level: ✓✓
Gently cook a small chopped onion for about 5 minutes without colouring in the butter. If you are serving the soup straight away, then retain eight asparagus tips for the garnish and blanch as in previous recipe. Roughly chop the rest of the asparagus spears and add them to the pan. Cover and sweat very gently for another 10 minutes, giving it a stir from time to time.
Sprinkle in a rounded teaspoon of plain flour, stir well and then gradually add the hot chicken stock, stirring all the time. Bring to simmering point and season with salt and black pepper. Cook very gently without boiling, partially covered, for 20 minutes.
Allow the soup to cool and then put it into a blender and whiz until smooth. Add the crème fraiche and whiz again. If you are going to serve this hot, gently re-heat (but do not boil), divide between your soup bowls and garnish with a blanched asparagus tip. If you're going to freeze the soup, then pour it into a plastic pot with a lid. To serve from frozen (either hot or cold), defrost, re-heat (if necessary) and garnish with a swirl of cream and a little dill.

Simplicity level: ✔

Mousse de Saumon Fumée
Mousse of Smoked Salmon

Presentation:
Amuse-bouche plates

Ingredients:
5oz/150g package of sliced
smoked salmon
1 small onion
2tbs crème fraiche/sour cream
1/2tsp/3ml white pepper
Juice of ½ lemon
8 bread sticks for garnish

This versatile mousse can be served with toast or used as a filling or topping for raw vegetables. Any good smoked salmon slices can be used. Just mix the ingredients in the food processor and you have a tasty treat. The ingredient measurements below are suggestions and can easily be adjusted to your taste. This mousse can be kept for several days as long as the salmon is not near its sell-by date.

Method:
Separate salmon slices and rough cut in pieces. Place it in the bowl of a food processor. Rough chop the onion and add to the processor bowl. Add crème fraiche, lemon juice, onion and white pepper. Process/pulse until the mixture is smooth and mousse-like. If necessary add more crème fraiche or lemon to add moisture and correct the seasoning.

Pavé de Saumon au Citron Vert

Salmon Morsel with Lime Sauce

Presentation:
Amuse-bouche plates

Ingredients:
7oz/200g raw salmon - cut to fit serving plate
Sauce:
2 tbs/15ml of butter
1-2 limes - juice and zest
1½cup/360ml cream or
1cup/240ml cream and
½cup/120ml crème fraiche

Although generally we serve this warm, it could be served at room temperature on a hot day. The salmon filet is cut into a 1inch/2.5cm square and about the same thickness. The salmon can be baked, poached or sautéed. A piece of bread for wiping the sauce is suggested. Ideally, infuse the butter and the lime zest for several hours or overnight. The finished sauce can be made a couple days ahead and chilled or frozen.

Method:
In a sauce pan, melt the butter on low. Add the lime zest. Turn off the heat and infuse the flavor for at least an hour or it can also sit in the fridge overnight. When you are ready to finish the sauce, heat it on low with the lime juice and cream. It should be a thick creamy texture. Correct the seasoning. You can also save the finished sauce in the fridge for a day or two.
Sautée the salmon squares till crispy and brown, then turn and finish.
Coat the serving dishes with sauce and top with salmon. Garnish with a twist of lime rind.

Saumon Fumé sur Crème de Concombre
Smoked Salmon on Cucumber Cream

Presentation:
Amuse-bouche spoon or dish

Ingredients:
Packaged smoked salmon slices or diced
½ cucumber
¼ cup salt and 2 cups water
Sour cream or crème fraiche - ½ cup to start and adjust so the cucumber is creamy
Few sprigs of fresh dill for garnish

If your guests do not eat salmon, the creamed cucumber can be served as a vegetarian amuse-bouche by simply garnishing with dill or chives to add a little color. It is best to start soaking the cucumber the day before you plan on serving it and the cucumber cream can be chilled and held in the fridge. The proportions below are not exact as the size of cucumbers vary as well as the quantity of cream the slices will absorb.

Method:
Peel and seed the cucumber by cutting it in half lengthwise and running a spoon down the center.

Cross slice the cucumber half into paper thin slices and place them in a bowl of very salty water.
Soak for a minimum of 1 hour but it is best left overnight covered in the fridge.
Drain the water and wring cucumber in a kitchen towel to remove the all the moisture. The cucumber will be limp and lack crispness.
In a bowl mix cream and cucumber and correct the seasoning (an option is to add some dill weed). Then chill till ready to serve.
Serve in a Chinese soup spoon and top with diced salmon or strips and garnish with a sprig of dill.

Coquilles Saint-Jacques Chinoises

Chinese Scallops

Presentation:
Pretty little saucers or amuse-bouche plates

Ingredients:
8 large fresh scallops
A knob of fresh ginger, grated
Juice of half a lemon
Chinese five spice mix
Small handful of fresh marjoram leaves
Knob or two of butter
Teaspoon of olive oil
Salt & pepper

Whenever they have those wonderful, big juicy scallops on 'special offer' at our local supermarket, I cannot resist them and this simple recipe makes a perfect amuse-bouche. For the gentlemen at your table it will probably be a one-bite wonder but we like to serve these giant scallops with a little fork for the ladies. You can prepare them earlier, cling-film/plastic wrap them and pop them in the fridge until you're ready to cook.
Tip: we keep our 'fresh' ginger frozen in the freezer in a little plastic bag. It's much easier to grate when it's frozen and you won't waste the rest. With a sharp knife, just peel off as much of the skin as you need and then grate.

Method:
Prepare the scallops by picking off any little black bits and wipe them dry. Score them with a sharp knife in a criss-cross pattern on one side only. Season lightly and then sprinkle them generously with your Chinese five spice mix. Cling film/plastic wrap and leave them in the fridge until you're ready to cook.
Melt the butter and the oil in a small frying pan until it's hot, add the grated ginger and then fry the scallops for two minutes until they turn a golden brown. Turn them over and cook for another minute. Slide them out of the pan on to your little saucers and then add the lemon juice, the marjoram leaves and a little more butter to the juices in the pan. Season with a generous grinding of pepper and a little salt. Allow the juices to bubble briefly and then pour a little liquid around each scallop and serve straight away.

Mangue aux Saint-Jacques
Mango with Scallops

Presentation:
Amuse-bouche spoons

Ingredients:
Jar of mango chutney
8 scallops (defrosted if frozen)
1 fresh ripe mango
2 teaspoons of curry powder
Butter for frying

If you have a lovely, ripe mango in the fruit bowl, mango chutney in the store cupboard and some scallops in the freezer, then you have the makings of a very easy but delicious amuse-bouche. If you have an Indian theme for your meal serve these little spoonfuls of magic between your starter and main course. You can prepare the spoons beforehand and allow the uncooked scallops to marinate in the curry powder for several hours; then all you have to do is flash-fry them before serving.

Method:
Put a tiny dollop of mango chutney in each spoon.
Peel and slice the mango into spoon size wedges and put a slice onto each spoon.
Pat the scallops dry and then press them into the curry powder to coat both sides.
Gently fry the scallops in a little butter for 1 minute each side.
Press one scallop onto each spoon and serve straight away.

St. Jacques sur Purée de Choux Fleur
Scallop on Cauliflower Purée

This unusual combination works surprisingly well. The bacon wrap is optional. Another choice is to crumble cooked bacon on top. You can prepare the cauliflower purée beforehand or even freeze it for later use.

Presentation:
Amuse-bouche spoon

Ingredients:
8 scallops - one each person
Cajun spice - sprinkle for each scallop
8 bacon slices to wrap around scallop or 4 slices cut in half, cooked for crumbles
¼ head cauliflower - thin sliced
Whole milk to cover cauliflower
Salt and white pepper
Butter and olive oil for cooking
Heavy/double cream
Chives - fine chopped for garnish

Method:
Put enough butter and olive oil in the bottom of a lidded sauté pan to cover it. Add the cauliflower and sweat a few minutes. Then cover with the milk and simmer covered until very soft. Add some cream if it seems to be getting too dry. Season with salt and pepper. Purée the mixture in small batches until velvety. It will be smoother if blended while still warm. At this point, it can be chilled, frozen or returned to the pan for use. Preheat the oven to 400F/200C. Sprinkle the top of each scallop with Cajun spice. Wrap the outside edge with a piece of bacon and secure with a cocktail stick. Place on a buttered baking pan and broil/grill for 6-8 minutes at 5 inches from the heat source until browned but not dried out (do not turn). If you plan to top the scallop with crumbled bacon instead of wrapping it, the bacon can be cooked on the same sheet with the scallops.
To serve, fill each spoon with warmed cauliflower purée and place a scallop on top so that the browned side is up. Top with bacon crumble or chopped chives.

St. Jacques avec Purée des Petits Pois à la Menthe

Scallops with Minted Pea Purée

This seems like a strange combination but the flavors work very well and the green pea color makes a lovely presentation. The pea mixture can be made well ahead of serving time and chilled. It is a good warm weather amuse-bouche.

Presentation:
Amuse-bouche bowl, small verrine or spoon

Ingredients:
1 large shallot, chopped
9oz/250g frozen baby peas
1oz/25g butter
10-12 fresh mint leaves, rough chopped
4oz/110ml chicken stock made with a bouillon cube
8 Bay scallops plus butter to wipe the skillet

Method:
Saute the shallot in the butter until soft but not brown. Add the chicken stock. Then add the mint and the peas. Bring to a boil and simmer no more than 5 minutes, until peas are soft but still bright green. Whiz the pea mixture in a food processor and then put through a food mill or sieve so that you have a velvety sauce. It can be chilled at this point and saved until ready to serve.

When ready to serve, remove the pea mixture from the fridge and divide between the amuse-bouche bowls. Pat dry the Bay scallops and sauté on medium in a skillet wiped with butter. When lightly browned, turn the scallops and cook a little longer, but do not overcook or they will be tough. They will also continue to cook a little after being removed from the skillet. Place a scallop on top of the pea mixture and serve with a spoon.

Salade d'Asperges, Avocat et Crevettes

Asparagus, Avocado and Shrimp/Prawn Salad

With the exception of blanching the asparagus tips, this amuse-bouche is easy to assemble. If available, purchase a shrimp for each person that has been cooked and peeled or poach your own. You can allow the ingredients to marinate for several hours and assemble them at the last minute. Everyone will love this little treat - three favorites all in one go!

Presentation:
Amuse-bouche plate

Ingredients:
8 green asparagus tips
8 shrimp
8 small slices of ripe avocado
Your favorite vinaigrette
Fresh minced coriander, chives or parsley for garnish

Method:
Cook the asparagus tips in boiling sugared water for 2 minutes and then plunge into cold water to keep its color. Let the tips dry on a towel
Cook the shrimp (if not prepared) and peel.
Peel the avocado, cut it in half and slice one half horizontally until you have 8 slices.
Marinate the asparagus, shrimp and avocado in a bowl with vinaigrette for a minimum of 10 minutes.
Arrange on dish and garnish with minced herbs.

Cocktail de Crevettes

Prawn Cocktail

Presentation:
Amuse-bouche verrines

Ingredients
24 plump cooked and peeled prawns/shrimp
8cm/2 inches of cucumber, diced
1 large tomato, diced (discard the pips)
2 tablespoons of crème fraiche
Tube of tomato purée
Salt & pepper
Fresh mint to garnish

This is our take on an old favourite. It's a lovely, fresh little amuse-bouche and quite harmless. You won't frighten your granny with this one; indeed she will love you forever if you serve it every time she comes to lunch! It looks very pretty too, so you will be awarded plenty of 'Brownie points' for presentation. It can be made up several hours before you serve it, preferably at the beginning of your meal.

Method:
Mix the crème fraiche with a squeeze or two of tomato purée to make a smooth, pale pink sauce. Season with salt and pepper to taste.
Pop the diced cucumber into the base of your verrine and then pile the diced tomato on top on the cucumber. Top with ground black pepper.
Mix 16 prawns/shrimp into the sauce and pile them into the verrine (allowing 2 prawns/shrimp per glass) on top of the tomato. Garnish with another prawn/shrimp and chill. When you are ready to serve, garnish with a little fresh mint.

Crevettes Piquantes au Tabasco

Piquant Prawns in a Tabasco Marinade

These lovely pickled prawns/shrimp need about 48 hours in the fridge for the flavour to come through. Buy nice, big raw prawns from your fishmonger (they will be grey in colour at this stage) and take off the heads and scaly body armour, but leave on the little tails to help your guests eat them in one 'amuse-bouche' mouthful

Presentation:
Amuse-bouche sauce dishes

Ingredients:
8 large raw prawns, peeled and be-headed. but leave the tails on
Quarter of a small green pepper, thinly sliced and finely chopped
Quarter of a small red pepper, thinly sliced and finely chopped
1 shallot thinly sliced and finely chopped
Wedge of lemon, finely chopped
1 teaspoon of drained capers
2 teaspoons of fruity olive oil
1 teaspoon wine vinegar
2 teaspoons of lime juice (you can use the squirty stuff in a plastic bottle if you like)
Half a small teaspoon of English mustard powder
Good shake of Worcestershire sauce
Good shake of Tabasco sauce
Salt and pepper
Half a teaspoon of sugar
Salad leaves for garnish

Method:
Put the prawns/shrimp in a small bowl with the peppers, shallot, lemon and capers. Mix together the olive oil, vinegar, lime juice, mustard powder, Worcester and Tabasco sauce, salt, pepper and sugar in a screw topped jar and give it a good shake. Pour it over the prawns, cover with clingfilm/plastic wrap and put the bowl in the fridge for about 48 hours to pickle. Give the mixture a stir from time to time. They should have turned pink by this time.
To serve, put a few salad leaves in your little dishes and then carefully place a prawn in each dish. Spoon over a little of the marinade mixture and juice. A crusty baguette is great to soak up all the lovely spicy juices.

'Green-eyed' Crevettes

'Green-eyed' Prawns/Shrimps

Presentation:
Amuse-bouche spoons

Ingredients for the green-eyed prawns/shrimps:
8 cooked and peeled jumbo prawns/shrimps
Jar of horseradish sauce
Tube of Wasabi purée
Small tub of crème fraiche
Freshly squeezed lemon juice
Salt & pepper
Thinly sliced lemon cut into tiny triangles

Ingredients for Crevette avec confiture de piment rouge:
8 cooked and peeled jumbo prawns/shrimps
8 large basil leaves
Crème fraiche
Sweet chilli jam (store cupboard/pantry recipe page 139)

These 'green-eyed' prawns/shrimps look spectacular and are so easy to make. They can be prepared a few hours before your meal and kept in the fridge until you're ready to serve. Prawns/shrimps are the perfect 'package' for amuse bouche and below we have another four 'spoon' ideas.

Method:
Put the prawns into a small bowl and squeeze the lemon over. Grind with black pepper and leave to marinate in the fridge for an hour or two.
Mix equal amounts of horseradish with crème fraiche and season lightly. Put a small teaspoon of the mixture onto each spoon. Place a prawn on top of the horseradish cream.

Squeeze a drop of Wasabi purée at the 'head' of each prawn.
Decorate with a lemon triangle and refrigerate until ready to serve

For Crevette avec confiture de piment rouge (with sweet chilli jam), pictured below:
Line each spoon with a basil leaf and put a small dollop of crème fraiche on each leaf. Press a prawn/shrimp into the crème fraiche. Dribble a small teaspoon of sweet chilli

à la Crème de Raifort

with Creamed Horseradish (and other recipes)

jam (see store cupboard recipe page 139) over the crevette before serving.

For Crevette d'oeufs de lump rouges et Petit Suisse* (with red caviar & Petit Suisse*) pictured below:
Cut two Petits Suisses into four equal circles and place each circle on a spoon (or a small, flat amuse bouche plate if you prefer). Add a small teaspoon of caviar and finish with a prawn/shrimp. Grind with black pepper and garnish with basil.

For Crevette au Curry (in a curry sauce) pictured bottom right:
Melt a teaspoon of butter with

2 teaspoons of oil in a pan and gently fry a chopped shallot. Add a teaspoon each of cumin powder, ground ginger, chilli powder and ground coriander, the seeds from 2 cardamon pods, half a teaspoon of turmeric, a clove of garlic (crushed) and fry for 2 minutes before adding a small carton of coconut milk. Cook very gently for about 10 minutes. You can prepare this earlier, but re-heat before serving. Divide the mixture between the spoons and then top with a prawn. Garnish with a little parsley and a tiny wedge of lemon.

Ingredients for Crevette d'oeufs de lump rouges et Petit Suisse:*
8 cooked and peeled jumbo prawns/shrimps
2 Petits Suisses*
Small pot of red lumpfish caviar
Black pepper and basil to garnish

Ingredients for Crevette au Curry: ✓✓
8 cooked and peeled jumbo prawns/shrimps
Butter & oil for frying
1 shallot, chopped
1tsp each of ground cumin, ginger, chilli & coriander
2 cardamon pods
½ tsp turmeric
1 clove garlic
200ml carton coconut milk
Pasley and lemon wedges to garnish

*Petit Suisse is a Normandy cream cheese that is sold in a pack of 6 small cylinders wrapped in paper or a tube, usually eaten as a dessert with honey or sugar. Other cream cheeses could be substituted.

Katsoa Tataki

Presentation:
Tiny glass square presentation dishes

Ingredients:
About 350g/12oz of really fresh tuna
1 tablespoon of sesame seeds
1 teaspoon of Chinese five spice mix
1 teaspoon of sesame oil
1 teaspoon of ginger pulp (or grated fresh ginger)
1 clove of garlic, crushed
Juice of half a lemon
Half a teaspoon of shrimp paste
1 teaspoon of soya sauce
1 shallot, finely chopped
Salt and pepper
Redcurrants to garnish

Seared Tuna with Ginger & Shrimp Paste

This is a traditional Asian taste that our French guests love. Spicy tastes are unusual in French cuisine but they are changing! You can sear the tuna (which must be very fresh) and make the tataki the day before but keep it covered and remember to allow the fish to soften a little from the freezer before you slice it. We garnished these Katsoa with pretty little bunches of fresh redcurrants but you can use any tiny fruit or even little triangles of sliced lemon, if that is all that is available.

Method:
Mix the sesame seeds with the five spice, salt and pepper. Cut the tuna into 1inch cubes (1 per person) and press each piece into the sesame seed mixture, coating every side. Oil and heat a griddle pan and when hot, sear the tuna pieces on each side for about 20 seconds until the seeds turn golden. Do not overcook. Remove from the heat and pop them in the freezer, which will stop them cooking and make them easier to slice.
Put the ginger, garlic, lemon, shrimp paste, soya sauce and shallot into a small bowl and mix well. Clingfilm/plastic wrap and put it in the fridge. Half an hour before you are ready to serve, put a small teaspoon of the mixture into each amuse-bouche dish. Take the tuna from the freezer, allow to soften a little and then with a sharp knife, slice each cube into three or four small slices. Each slice should be rare in the centre with a seared sesame edge. Arrange the slices on top of the tataki mixture and garnish with the redcurrants. Allow to rest before serving.

Note: Use balsamic glaze rather than balsamic vinegar to make your bread dips. The glaze will hold its shape when you add the oil (use a fruity olive oil infused with a garlic clove or some chilli oil - see store cupboard recipes).

Cubes de Thon au Basilic

Tuna Cube with Basil

For the cubes, the tuna is marinated in a heavenly Mediterranean dressing and then lightly steamed in sorrel leaves - or basil leaves, if your plant has some giant leaves. The tuna must be very fresh. You can make the marinade beforehand and add the fish up to four hours before to soak up those gorgeous flavours.

Presentation:
Amuse-bouche plastic or glass cubes or spoons

Ingredients:
300g/10oz chunk of really fresh tuna
Small handful of basil leaves
Small handful of parsley, leaves picked
1 large garlic clove
Grated zest and juice of half a lemon
1 tablespoon olive oil
Half a teaspoon of salt
Black pepper
Sorrel leaves or large basil leaves

Method (cubes):
Put the basil, parsley, garlic, lemon juice and zest, olive oil, salt and pepper into a blender and whiz until nearly smooth. Cut the tuna into 1cm/half inch cubes and cover with the marinade. Clingfilm and keep cool in the fridge for up to four hours.
Scrape the marinade from each cube and retain. Loosen it with a little olive oil if necessary. Carefully fold the fish up in the leaves into neat little cubes and allow to rest in the fridge until you're ready to steam.
When your steamer is hot, steam the fish for 2-3 minutes and then carefully place each one into a presentation cube or spoon with the aid of a pair of tongs. Put a dollop of the marinade on top of each tuna cube. Serve with a cocktail stick.

Cuillères de Ton

Tuna Spoons

Presentation:
Amuse-bouche spoons

Ingredients for the the spoons:
200g/7oz chunk of really fresh
tuna
1 shallot, finely chopped
2 teaspoons lemon juice
2 teaspoons lime juice
2 sorrel leaves
Half a teaspoon of salt
Black pepper
Pesto Mayonaise (see store
cupboard/pantry recipe on
page 137)

For these spoons, the tuna must be very fresh as it isn't cooked but simply marinated in the salt, lemon and lime juice. You can make the marinade beforehand but don't combine with the fish until about half an hour before serving.

Method for the spoons:
Using a pair of sharp kitchen scissors, cut the tuna into very small pieces. In a bowl, add the tuna to a finely chopped shallot and a few shredded sorrel leaves, as well as 2 teaspoons each of lemon and lime juice and the salt. Season with black pepper and mix well. Cover with clingfilm/plastic wrap and chill for at least 15 minutes, but no more than half an hour.

When the fish has marinated, put about half a teaspoon of pesto mayonnaise (see store cupboard recipes on page 137) in each amuse-bouche spoon and then, using your fingers, mould a good dollop of the tuna mix on top.

Viandes & Volailles
Meat & Poultry

Beef

Concombre et Boeuf Pacquets   87
Cucumber and Beef Parcels

Roti de Boeuf et 'Yorkshire Pudding'   88
Roast Beef and Yorkshire Pudding

Roulade de Boeuf avec Glace au Parmesan   89
Beef Roll with Parmesan Ice Cream

Chicken

Foie de Volaille avec Gelée de Cumberland   90
Chicken Paté with Cumberland Jelly

Mini 'Cornish Pasties'   91
Mini Cornish Pasties

Poulet Fumé au Bleu   92
Smoked Chicken with Blue Cheese Fondant

Samosas de Poulet Fumé à la Sauce Aigre-douce   93
Smoked Chicken Samosas with Sweet & Sour Sauce

Duck

Rouleaux de Canards à la Pekinoise   95
Duck Roll Peking Style

Foie Gras

Crème de Foie Gras Caramélisée   96
Caramelized Foie Gras Cream

Crème de Foie Gras au Porto et Parmesan   97
Foie Gras Cream with Port and Parmesan

Croutons au Foie Gras avec Confiture d'Oignons   98
Butter Croutons with Foie Gras on an Onion Marmalade

Flûtes au Foie Gras   99
Filo Tubes of Foie Gras

Ham

'Grits' au Fromage et Jambon   100
Cheese Grits with Ham

Tartes Miniatures   101
Small Tarts with Bacon or Ham

Rouleau de Printemps au Jambon Cru   102
Asian Spring Roll with Ham

Sausage/Sausage Meat

Brochette de Boulettes de Viande   103
Meatball on a Skewer

'Toad in the Hole'   104
Toad in the Hole

Canelloni/Manicotti Farcis à la Viande ou au Fromage   105
Canelloni/Manicotti with Meat or Cheese Filling

Champignon Farci à la Saucisse   106
Sausage Stuffed Mushroom

Concombre et Boeuf Paquets

Cucumber and Beef Parcels

Presentation:
Amuse-bouche presentation plates or cubes
Cocktail sticks

Ingredients:
1 cucumber, halved
1 large fillet steak
Jar of horseradish
Small tub of crème fraiche
Tube of wasabi
Salt and pepper
Parsley to garnish

Store Cupboard/Pantry:
Fresh tomato sauce (see page 134)

Fillet steak/filet mignon is very expensive but just one thick steak will do for up to eight people, so it isn't too extravagant to make these little parcels. The beef must be very tender so it is important to use a good cut of meat. You can prepare the amuse-bouche the day before but assembly should take place an hour or so before the meal. It is really rather special, so we suggest you serve it at the beginning of the meal when everyone is hungry!

Method:
Using a very sharp knife or vegetable parer, cut long, paper-thin slices of cucumber from top to bottom, trying to make sure you have a thin green edge on each slice and avoiding the seeded centre. Soak the slices overnight in a brine solution (1 part salt to 4 parts water) to soften and season.

Cut the fillet steak into the appropriate number of cubes (they shouldn't be bigger than a mouthful). Season and fry very briefly (less than a minute), moving them around to seal each side. You want the meat to still be pink in the middle. Drain on kitchen roll. Cover with clingfilm/plastic wrap and chill.

To prepare the parcel, place the cucumber slices on some kitchen roll and pat dry. Spread a little Horseradish down the centre of each slice and then roll each beef cube up in the cucumber as shown. Put a small teaspoon of fresh tomato sauce in the bottom of your presentation dish and then carefully place a parcel on top. Squeeze a small blob of wasabi on the top of each and garnish with parsley. Serve with a cocktail stick.

Roti de Boeuf et 'Yorkshire Pudding'
Roast Beef and Yorkshire Pudding

Presentation:
Amuse-bouche presentation plates
Cupcake paper moulds

Ingredients:
2-3 very rare slices of cold roast beef, cut into small squares.
75g/3oz plain flour
1 egg
75m/3 fl oz milk
55ml/2 fl oz water
Salt and pepper
Oil for cooking
Jar of hot horseradish
Bottle of balsamic glaze
Parsley to garnish

Here is our take on a truly British dish, amuse-bouche style! If you have cooked roast beef for your Sunday lunch, then save a small piece to make these gorgeous little buns. You can make the Yorkshire puddings several days before, but store in an air tight tin when they are completely cold. Do not assemble too early otherwise the puds will go soggy - and serve at room temperature.

Method:
Pre-heat the oven to 220 degrees C.
Put half a teaspoon of oil into each mould in a patty tin and pop the tin into the hot oven for 5 minutes before you are ready to add the batter.
Sift the flour with the salt and pepper into a bowl and using an electric whisk, beat in the egg. Gradually add the milk and water to form a smooth batter.
When the oil is sizzling, divide the batter between the moulds and return the tin to the oven as quickly as possible.
Cook for about 15-20 minutes until well risen, crisp and golden.
Cool on a wire rack.
When completely cold, using a pair of sharp kitchen scissors, snip each bun half way through and fill with a small teaspoon of Horseradish and then a slice of beef, folded into a triangle, so that it is slightly larger than the bun.
Squeeze a good dollop of balsamic glaze onto the top of each bun.
Place the buns into cupcake paper moulds and serve at room temperature, garnished with a little parsley.

Roulade de Boeuf avec Glace au Parmesan

Beef Roll with Parmesan Ice Cream

This amuse-bouche is good for using up some leftovers. It can be made with leftover rice and a paper thin slice of steak, preferably cooked rare or medium rare, or a slice of carpaccio. The Parmesan ice cream and crisp, combined with the beef, reminds us of Italy. Use a high quality Parmesan to give the most flavor. For ease, you can make the ice cream and crisp a couple of days ahead.

Method:
Mix the rice with horseradish cream. Correct seasoning.
Put the rice on a slice of beef and roll overlapping the ends for closure.
Place sealed side down on the dish.
Sprinkle the top with a little minced parsley/coriander and a drop of horseradish.
Put the Parmesan ice cream in a bowl or glass next to the beef roll.
Garnish with a Parmesan crisp.

Parmesan Ice Cream:
8oz/250g good quality grated Parmesan
2cups/450ml heavy cream
2 egg whites
In a sauce pan, cook whole cream and grated parmesan(6oz/150g) until blended and smooth. Whisk the egg whites. Stir the remaining Parmesan into the warm mixture and fold in the egg whites. Freeze in individual serving dishes or in a tight container and then scoop to serve.

Parmesan Crisp:
The amount of cheese per crisp depends on the size you want. A 2 inch diameter works well. Fresh grated cheese works better than pre-packaged grated Parmesan. Put the grated cheese in a round on a baking tray covered with baking paper. We find that the fresh grated cheese should be about a half inch thick on the outside edge to hold its shape and can be thinner in the center. Bake in the oven or toaster oven until the cheese has melted. The

Presentation:
Amuse-bouche flat dish, large enough to hold the beef roll, a small dish for an ice cream ball and a knife, fork and spoon on the side

Beef Roll Ingredients:
8 thin slices of beef about 3x2 inches
8 tbsp cooked rice
4 tsp horseradish cream or to taste
Fine chopped parsley or coriander leaf for garnish
Salt and pepper to taste

baking period is just a few minutes and requires your attention so as not to burn. Let cool and solidify, then remove them from the paper. The rounds will keep fresh in a tight container and can be used to accompany or garnish other dishes such as soups.

Foies de Volailles avec Gelée de Cumberland

Chicken Paté with Cumberland Jelly

A delicious, rich paté which melts in the mouth. The addition of whipped cream makes it lighter than normal. These are a more substantial amuse-bouche and might follow a light, summer soup and before a main fish course. Keep any left-over paté for lunch the next day. The paté can be prepared well in advance (indeed the flavour improves over 24 hours) but do not spoon out the Cumberland jelly until the last minute, because it will melt. Serve with tiny slices of toasted brioche or sesame baguette.

Presentation:
Pretty petits pots or spoons
Amuse-bouche sauce dishes
Amuse-bouche plates
Tiny cake knives

Ingredients:
300g/11 oz chicken or duck livers, sinew and fat removed
2 small shallots finely chopped
1 clove garlic, crushed
125g/4½ oz salted butter
1 tablespoons port
50ml/2 oz double cream
Salt & pepper
Roughly ground black peppercorns
Thin slices of lemon, cut into tiny triangles

Store Cupboard/Pantry:
Cumberland jelly (page 133)

Method:

Melt 50g/2 oz of butter in a small frying pan and add the livers, shallots and garlic. Season well with salt and pepper. Fry very gently for about 6 minutes, until the livers are sealed. Turn up the heat and add the port. Let the mixture bubble for a minute.

Allow to cool a little and then whiz through the blender, adding 25g/1 oz of butter, cubed.

Whip the double cream and fold it into the mixture. Taste, and add more salt if necessary. Tip a spoonful into each pot, level the surface and allow to set in the fridge.

Set your pepper grinder so that it grinds the black peppercorns into largish chunks and add a twist or two onto the surface of each pot. Clarify the remaining butter by gently melting it. When it separates, pour off the clear butter into a small jug, using the blade of a knife to keep back the milky solids. Spoon a little of the clarified butter over each pot and return to the fridge.

When you're ready to serve, put each pot onto an amuse-bouche plate and a teaspoon of Cumberland jelly into each sauce dish. Decorate with a tiny triangle of lemon and serve immediately.

Mini 'Cornish Pasties'
Mini Cornish Pasties

Traditionally, Cornish pasties were baked as an all-in-one lunch for the Cornish farmers and miners. One end would have a savoury filling and the other end would be the 'dessert' with a sweet filling of jam or fruit. Our take on this are tiny two-bite pasties with a spicy chicken filling at one end and a sweet and sour pineapple filling at the other. They look great and they taste great. You can prepare the pasties beforehand and allow them to rest in the fridge until you are ready to bake.

Method:

Pre-heat oven to 200C/400F. Mix the curry powder with the lemon juice in a small bowl. Heat some oil in a small pan and add the chopped shallot. Fry gently until softened. Add the garlic, ginger and curry mixture and stir over a gentle heat for a few minutes. Add the chicken, the coriander, seasoning and the wine. Stir, and allow to simmer very gently for about 5 minutes or until all the wine has been absorbed. Allow to cool. Roll out the shortcrust pastry and cut circles with a 7cm pastry cutter or glass. Moisten the edge of each circle with a little beaten egg and then pile about half a teaspoon of the chicken mixture in the centre at one end (but not too near the edge) and half a teaspoon of sweet and sour sauce on the other end. Carefully pull up the sides and pinch them together, making sure that the ends of the pasty are firmly closed. We found it helps if you flour your fingers to prevent them sticking to the pastry. Place them on a piece of baking parchment on an oven tray and glaze them with a little beaten egg. Pop into the oven for about 10-12 minutes until golden brown. Place a pasty on each-amuse bouche plate and garnish with a basil leaf or some parsley. Serve straight away.

Presentation:
Amuse-bouche presentation plates
Amuse-bouche sauce dishes

Ingredients (makes about 16 - allow 2 each or freeze the other 8):
Packet of shortcrust pastry
60g/2½ oz of finely chopped smoked chicken
1 teaspoon of butter
1 teaspoon of oil
1 shallot, finely chopped
1 clove of garlic, crushed
1 knob of ginger, peeled and grated, straight from the freezer (or fresh)
1 teaspoon of curry powder
2 teaspoons of lemon juice
Chopped coriander
Small glass of white wine
Olive oil for cooking
Salt & pepper
1 beaten egg

Store Cupboard/Pantry:
Sweet and sour pineapple sauce (see page 138)

Poulet Fumé au Bleu

Presentation:
Amuse-bouche spoons
Amuse-bouche presentation plates

Ingredients
1-2 thin slices of smoked chicken breast with skin
50g/2 oz creamy blue cheese (St Agur, Roquefort, etc)
3 heaped teaspoons crème fraiche
Crispy lettuce
Slice of fresh orange
Fresh orange wedge to squeeze

Smoked Chicken with Blue Cheese Fondant

This is simple to prepare, although a little fiddly to assemble - but it's worth it because the combined textures are heavenly. You can assemble the amuse-bouche several hours before the meal and chill in the fridge. Served first, perhaps with a small glass of chilled rosé Touraine wine, it's full of flavour and will have your guests panting for the next course.

Method:
Put the cheese and the crème fraiche into a small bowl and mash together until you have a creamy consistency.
Finely shred some crispy lettuce.
Carefully fill the base of each amuse-bouche spoon with a little shredded lettuce.

Press a level teaspoon of the cheese mixture onto the lettuce.
Cut small wedges of the chicken breast to fit each spoon and tuck into the side of the spoon, skin side up.
Cut a thin slice of orange, removed peel and pith and cut into tiny wedges. Arrange a wedge at the base of each spoon.
Cut a wedge or two of orange and squeeze it over the amuses-bouches before serving.

Samosas de Poulet Fumé à la Sauce Aigre-douce
Smoked Chicken Samosas with Sweet and Sour Sauce

A perfect introduction to a meal with an Indian theme - or just use these tasty amuse-bouches to spice up your meal in between courses. If you haven't made samosas with filo pastry before, then cut a piece of paper to the size indicated below and practice folding into little triangles. It is important that all sides of the samosas are sealed. You can prepare them in advance and pop them in the fridge until you're ready to cook. Serve with mango chutney or our store cupboard Sweet & Sour Sauce.

Method:
Pre-heat oven to 200C/400F. Mix the curry powder with the lemon juice in a small bowl. Heat some oil in a small pan and add the chopped shallot. Fry gently until softened. Add the garlic, ginger and curry mixture and stir over a gentle heat for a few minutes. Add the chicken, the coriander, seasoning and the wine. Stir, and allow to simmer very gently for about 5 minutes or until all the wine has been absorbed. Allow to cool.
Cut 6cm x 18cm/2½ x 7 inch strips of filo pastry
Melt the butter and oil in the microwave for about 20 seconds and lightly brush each strip of pastry as you work.
Put a small teaspoon of the chicken mixture at the start of the pastry strip and fold into a triangle. Keep folding until you have a neat little samosa triangle. Repeat until you have used up the chicken mixture. Place the samosas on a baking tray lined with baking parchment. Chill if required. Before you pop them in the oven, lightly brush the surface with the rest of the melted butter and oil.
Bake for 6/7 minutes until golden brown. Serve immediately with our sweet and sour pineapple sauce (see page 138).

Presentation:
Amuse-bouche presentation plates
Amuse-bouche sauce dishes

Ingredients (makes about 16 - allow 2 each or freeze 8):
Packet of filo pastry
60g/2 ½oz of finely chopped smoked chicken
1 teaspoon of butter
1 teaspoon of oil
1 shallot, finely chopped
1 clove of garlic, crushed
1 knob of ginger, peeled and grated, straight from the freezer (or fresh)
1 teaspoon of curry powder
2 teaspoons of lemon juice
Chopped coriander
Small glass of white wine
Olive oil for cooking
Salt & pepper

Store Cupboard/Pantry:
Sweet and sour pineapple sauce (see page 138)

'Grits au Fromage et Jambon - see page 100

94

Rouleaux de Canards à la Pékinoise

Duck Roll Peking Style

This recipe is inspired by the Chinese dish Peking Duck, which is sliced and rolled in a pancake with onion, cucumber and seasoned with Hoisin sauce. It would be perfect for any leftover duck bits. With a little cutting and assembly you have an easy amuse-bouche which can be plastic-wrapped and chilled 2 hours ahead.

Presentation:
Amuse-bouche plate

Ingredients:
8oz/250g Leftover duck or uncooked boneless duck breast
8 Chinese pancakes approximately 6 inches diameter or substitute flour tortillas and cut to size
Jar of Hoisin sauce
4 scallions/spring onions cut in matchsticks
½ medium cucumber peeled, seeded and cut in matchsticks
Coriander/cilantro leaf for garnish (optional)

Method:
To cook a duck breast: (you could marinate the duck breast in Chinese flavors before cooking but it's not essential) score the skin side of the duck breast with a knife and place skin side down in a preheated nonstick fry pan for about 10 minutes. Keep removing the fat and when the skin is browned and thin, turn the breast over for another 5-10 minutes. Do not overcook the duck. It should be pink. Thin slice and cut into strips.
Lay out a pancake and spread it with some Hoisin sauce. Top with the duck, several onion and cucumber sticks. Roll and secure with a cocktail stick/skewer if necessary. Garnish with coriander/cilantro. Serve on a plate with a small dish of Hoisin sauce for dipping.

Crème de Foie Gras Caramélisée
Caramelized Foie Gras Cream

Presentation:
Amuse-bouche miniature crème brulée ramekin or ceramic tart dish, knife

Ingredients:
6-7oz/180g prepared foie gras
Sweet wine or liqueur - Sauterne, Poire William (Proportions of perhaps 2 oz/60g foie gras to 1 teaspoon wine)
8 tsp/5ml cream
8 tblsp/120ml approximate of brown sugar to cover top of your dish

This recipe is a play on the dessert of vanilla custard topped with caramelized sugar called Crème Brulée. The foie gras has a creamy consistency and a crunch on top. The foie gras can be whipped ahead of time and chilled but remove from the fridge a little before caramelizing. This is lovely served with a few sips of Sauterne.

Method:
Whip the foie gras and liqueur with a mixer. Finish with a bit of cream. It should have the consistency of a crème brulée. Correct the seasoning to your taste. Spread evenly in the serving dish. Sprinkle the top with sieved brown sugar and pass under the broiler/grill or use a cook's torch to caramelize. Serve with toast rounds.

Crème de Foie Gras au Porto et Parmesan

Foie Gras Cream with Port and Parmesan

Serve this amuse-bouche in a glass so the three layers are visible. It makes an unusual and attractive combination. Foie gras has an affinity for a sweet wine so the Port should be of the sweet variety, or you could substitute a Sauterne. Also the Parmesan topping should be subtle so as not to overwhelm the gorgeous foie gras. The Port jelly has to set, so you can start preparing this dish the day before your party.

Presentation:
Amuse-bouche glass

Ingredients:
8oz/225g foie gras - mousse or block that you whip with cream
8oz/250ml cream - adjust the cream amount for the moisture in your foie gras
8oz/250ml ruby Port
2tbs/30ml gelatin soaked in 1/4/60ml cup cold water
6oz/190ml Parmesan cheese - preferably freshly grated
1/2cup/125ml boiling water for the gelatin
8 -16 toast rounds

Method:
Prepare the foie gras into a mousse by beating 4oz/125ml cream into it with a mixer. Place it equally divided into each serving glass and chill.
Soak the gelatine in 1/4 cup/60ml cold water then dissolve it in the boiling water and add it to the Port which you have gently heated and allow the mixture to cool before pouring a little on the foie gras in each serving dish. Chill for at least 4 hours or until the Port jelly has set.
Heat the remaining 4oz/125ml of cream and the Parmesan until the cheese has melted and the cream reduced. Then beat the cream mixture and when cool, place on top of the Port jelly.

Garnish with a Parmesan shaving and serve with toast rounds. Or, you may chill till serving time. Garnish with a shaving of Parmesan and serve.

Croutons au Foie Gras avec Confiture d'Oignons

Butter Croutons with Foie Gras on an Onion Marmalade

Presentation:
Amuse-bouche presentation plates

Ingredients:
Small tin of foie gras, chilled
2-3 slices of yesterday's bread
Butter
A few black/redcurrants

Store cupboard/pantry:
Onion marmalade (see page 136)

A mouthful of perfection! AND it's all very simple. You will need a tiny pastry cutter or similar tool with a 3-4cm/1¼ inch diameter to cut the bread and the foie gras; we used the rim of a little rose vase. Make a few pots of our store cupboard onion marmalade; it keeps for ages and is perfect with foie gras - and lots of other things too. Use any edible berry in the garden to decorate; we used blackcurrants but perhaps redcurrants would be prettier. You can make these up a few hours in advance, but chill in the fridge.

Method:
Pre-heat the oven to 200 degrees C/400F. Lightly butter the slice of bread and then cut out 8 little circles with your chosen

tool. Bake in the oven for about 5 minutes until golden brown.
Next, take the tin of foie gras out of the fridge and open at both ends. Push the foie gras out of the tin onto a plate and using a wire cutter or sharp knife, cut a slice approximately 1cm/½ inch or less in thickness. Using the same tool that you used for the bread, cut the same number of circles of foie gras. Pinch together the scraps to make another circle or two. Chill.
When the croutons are cool, spread a little onion marmalade on each one.
Place a foie gras circle on each crouton and decorate with a berry.

Flûtes au Foie Gras

Filo Tubes filled with Foie Gras

Presentation:
Amuse-bouche presentation plates
Sauce dishes

Ingredients:
Small tin of foie gras, chilled in the fridge for several hours
Packet of filo pastry
Teaspoon each of butter and oil, melted in the microwave for 20 seconds

Foie gras is special in its own right, but baked in filo pastry it becomes even more special. Served with our store cupboard/pantry chilli jam for dipping, it makes a delicious amuse-bouche. For best results prepare the tubes before cooking and chill in the fridge. We made twists and baby samosas, too but the tubes were the most successful.

Store cupboard/pantry:
Chilli jam (see page 139)

Method:
Pre-heat the oven to 200 degrees C/ 400F. Open the tin of foie gras at both ends and push the foie gras out onto a plate. Cut 2 x 1cm/½ inch slices using a wire cutter and cut each into 5 slices lengthwise (you can use the round end bits to make a couple of extra flutes). Chill. Cut strips of filo pastry 12 cm/5 inches wide and 14 cm/6 inches long and brush each strip with the   melted oil. Place a slice of foie gras at one end of the pastry and tightly roll up to form a tube. Lightly brush the tube with the oil. Place the tubes onto a sheet of baking parchment and bake for 6-7 minutes until the tubes are golden brown. Allow two per person and serve straight from the oven with a tiny dish of chilli jam.

"Grits" au Fromage et Jambon
Cheese Grits with Ham

Presentation:
Amuse-bouche spoon or dish, warmed

Ingredients:
1cup/225g grits - boxed in most grocery stores in USA or substitute polenta
Cream or milk as per the box directions
½cup/110g or more of sharp cheese such as Cheddar
Salt and pepper
Black Forest type ham - julienned in small strips for garnish
½cup/110g brewed coffee (optional)

Grits has its roots in Native American culture and is a popular food in the southern United States where it is eaten creamed, baked or fried for any meal of the day, but most often at breakfast. It comes from white ground corn or hominy and its closest European equivalent is polenta.
This amuse-bouche is especially usable before a southern style dinner of fried chicken or fish, gumbo or jambalaya. It also could be used before a breakfast or a brunch.

Method:
Follow the cooking directions on the box of grits or polenta. Using cream as the liquid gives a richer flavor. Mix in a strong Cheddar type cheese until melted and creamy. Transfer the cheese grits to your amuse-bouche dish and top with fried juliennes of ham. If you want to be truly traditional, deglaze the ham pan with coffee and put a few drops on top before serving.

*Tip: If making with polenta, an optional cheese to use is Italian Gorgonzola

Tartes Miniatures

Small Tarts

Presentation:
Amuse-bouche tart dish or plate

Ingredients:
Tart pastry
Bacon & Mushroom:
2-3 slices bacon
Pat of butter
Several chopped mushrooms
2tbsp chopped onion
2 oz/60g shredded Swiss cheese
2 eggs
4 oz/100g crème fraiche
Ham & Tomato:
2 oz/60g Black Forest ham or prosciutto
8 slices of tomato the diameter of the tart
2 garlic cloves
2 oz/60g olive oil
Thyme & basil fine chopped for garnish

Buy a pre-made pie or tart pastry and you can prepare this amuse-bouche very quickly. The filling ideas are almost limitless and the tarts can be made a day ahead and reheated to serve. If you do not have miniature tart pans, a muffin tin can be used. Cut the pastry so it only comes an inch/3cm up the sides of the tin.

Method:
Heat the oven to 375F/190C. Cut the pastry in rounds to fit your molds.
Bacon & Mushroom:
Beat the eggs with the crème fraiche. Fry bacon till crisp. Drain and crumble. In the same pan, add the butter and sauté the chopped mushrooms until the liquid has evaporated. Mix with the rest of the ingredients. Put a spoon of bacon mix into the mold, add a spoon of egg mixture and bake for 20 minutes.

Ham & Tomato:
Combine the garlic, half the oil, ham and fresh black pepper in a food processor for 5 seconds. Place mixture in molds and top with a thin slice of tomato. Drizzle with oil and a touch of thyme. Bake for 18 minutes. Remove from oven and top with basil.

Serve on an amuse-bouche plate or in the tart baking dish.

Rouleau de Printemps au Jambon Cru

Asian Spring Roll with Ham

Presentation:
Amuse-bouche spoon and cocktail stick

Ingredients:
Rice paper
⅛ lb/60g ham
Fresh coriander/cilantro leaves to taste
2 garlic cloves
¼ tsp/2ml fresh ground pepper
⅓ cup/90ml olive oil
Bottle of Nem or Egg Roll dipping sauce

Asian inspired flavors are a nice surprise even with a typical western meal and this variation on the spring roll will work with almost any cuisine. Jambon Cru is a ham similar to Black Forest ham or Prosciutto. It is hard to give proportions when making individual servings in different size dishes, but if you have left over ham mixture, you can freeze it, or use it to create your own amuse-bouche. The ham mixture is similar to and could be used in the recipe for "Tartes Miniature" (see page 101)

Method:
Place the ham, garlic, olive oil and ground pepper in a food processor and grind to a paste. Add the coriander/cilantro leaves and pulse to mix.
Put the rice paper on a chopping board and cover with a moist towel. Cut into 2 inch by 1½ inch pieces or to fit your dish.
Place the ham mixture on the rice paper. Fold up the ends and roll.
Pour dipping sauce to cover the bottom of your spoon and place the ham roll seam side down. Garnish with a cilantro leaf and cocktail stick. Serve quickly.
If you need to make them ahead of time, cover tightly with plastic wrap/clingfilm so that the rice paper does not dry out and chill until serving time.

Brochette de Boulettes de Viande
Meatball on a Skewer

These meatballs can be served with many different sauces. Some suggestions are BBQ, sweet and sour, yogurt with ground cumin, soy and ginger, spiced coarse salt, vinegar, or mustard. Another option is to serve them wrapped in lettuce or cabbage with a Thai sauce. They can also be frozen cooked or uncooked and reheated. So, you can prepare these well in advance.

Presentation:
Amuse-bouche dish or small cup

Ingredients:
½lb/225g ground veal and pork
1 slice white bread - crust removed
⅛ cup/30ml milk - enough to soften bread
2 pressed garlic cloves
1tsp/5ml each of crushed fennel seed, rubbed sage, and assorted spices to taste (spice mix might consist of a pinch of onion salt, celery powder, thyme, paprika)
1 egg beaten
Salt and pepper
Oil for sautéing

Method:
In a bowl soften the bread with milk and squeeze out the excess liquid. Add the bread, the meat, the spices and the egg. Mix with your hands and form into 1in/2.5cm balls. Sauté in oil in small batches so all sides are browned (keeping them warm in the oven).
Serve the sauce of your choice (see suggestions above) in a small cup for dipping and rest the skewered meatball across the top. Optionally, place a piece of lettuce on a plate, top with a meatball and some sauce on the side. Invite your guests to fold the lettuce around the meatball.

'Toad in the Hole'

Toad in the Hole

Presentation:
Amuse-bouche plates

Ingredients (makes up to 12 mini Yorkshire puddings):
75g/3 oz plain flour
1 egg
75 ml/3 fl oz milk
55 ml/2 fl oz water
2 Merguez chipolatas
1 tablespoon of crème fraiche
1 tablespoon of grainy mustard
Olive oil
Salt & pepper

Our amuse-bouche take on this old family favourite is quite delicious. We used French Merguez chipolatas which are a choritzo-based fresh sausage but if you can't get these, then any spicy sausage will do. Your guests should be encouraged to pick the little Yorkshire puddings up in their fingers, and dip them into the mustard sauce. You can make the batter and mustard sauce beforehand, cover and leave in the fridge, but the rest of the recipe requires cooking just before you serve.

Method:
Pre-heat the oven to 220 degrees C/425F.
Sift the flour with the salt and pepper into a bowl and make a small well in the centre. Break the egg into it and using an electric whisk gradually add the milk and water to form a smooth batter.
Cut the sausages into small pieces to fit the bottom of each mould in your patty tin. Place a drop or two of olive oil and a piece of sausage in each mould and pop the tin into the oven whilst it is heating up for about 5 minutes to release the fat from the sausages.
When the fat is sizzling and your oven is up to heat, pour the batter evenly between the 12 moulds and return the tin to the oven as quickly as possible.
Cook for about 15 minutes until risen, crisp and golden.
Whilst the puddings are cooking, mix the crème fraiche and the grainy mustard together in a small bowl and divide the mixture between your amuse bouche plates to form a circle in the centre.
Place one pudding on each plate on top of the mustard and serve immediately.

Canelloni/Manicotti Farcis à la Viande ou au Fromage

Canelloni or Manicotti with Meat or Cheese Filling

Canelloni and Manicotti are tubular pastas that are large enough to stuff. For an amuse-bouche portion, stuff one or two tubes and slice. Two recipes for stuffing options can be found below. Serve with a homemade tomato sauce (see store cupboard recipe page 134) or a purchased one. You can cook and stuff the pasta beforehand, top with the sauce and then bake for half an hour or so before serving.

Presentation:
Amuse Bouche plate

Ingredients:
4 Canelloni or Manicotti tubes - will give you 8 halves. Use fewer tubes if you want smaller slices
Cheese stuffing:
1 egg yolk
8 oz/125g ricotta cheese
2 oz/60g chopped spinach (optional)
2 oz/60g Parmesan
Pinch nutmeg, salt

Meat stuffing:
8 oz/125g seasoned sausage, 1 egg yolk
3tblsp/45ml bread crumbs
6 chopped mushrooms (optional)
1cup/240ml tomato sauce
Additional grated Parmesan for garnish

Method:
Cook the pasta in salted water until tender but 'al dente' and dip in cold water. Drain and cool on a towel. Heat the oven to 400F/200C.
Cheese stuffing:
Beat the egg yolk and mix with the rest of the ingredients. Stuff the mixture into the cannelloni.
Meat stuffing:
Beat the egg yolk and mix with the rest of the ingredients. Stuff the mixture into the cannelloni.
Place the cannelloni close together in a single layer in a buttered baking dish. Top with the sauce and Parmesan. Bake for 10-15 minutes and cool for 5 minutes before slicing. Slice each cannelloni in half. Put a portion on each serving dish and top with sauce. Garnish with basil or parsley before serving.

Champignon Farci à la Saucisse
Sausage Stuffed Mushroom

Presentation:
Amuse-bouche plate
Miniature skewer optional

Ingredients:
8 medium mushroom caps or
16 small
8oz/225g ground sausage
with lot of flavor
1tblsp soy sauce
1tblsp Worcestershire sauce
1tblsp butter
1tbslp olive oil

There are many choices of sausage for the stuffing. Our preference is a ground pork sausage with sage flavoring. If you feel adventuresome, try making your own by purchasing ground pork and adding herbs and spices. Some optional seasonings are sage, garlic, thyme, onion, fennel seed, Cajun spice, paprika, and what your inventive mind finds on the spice shelf.

Method:
Remove the mushroom stem and brush off any dirt. Melt the butter with the oil in sauce pan and add the Worcestershire and soy. This combination adds great flavor to the mushrooms. Swirl the mixture together and add mushrooms, stem side up. Sautée gently until brown and turn over. Do not over-cook. If you want to go this far ahead of time, turn the caps stem side up and cool in pan.
When you're ready to serve, fill the stem hole in the cap with sausage and put them in the oven until the sausage is cooked - 5 or 10 minutes at 400F/200C depending on the amount of sausage. Serve hot.

Fromage
Cheese

Cream Cheese
Fromage Frais avec Confiture de Jalepeno
Cream Cheese with Jalepeno Jelly or Sweet Chilli Jam

108

Feta
Feta Marinée au Fenouil et Sésame
Fennel and Sesame Marinated Feta

109

Goats Cheese
Mini-pizza au Chèvre
Mini Goats Cheese Pizza

110

Tomate Cerise Farcie au Chèvre
Cherry Vine Tomatoes stuffed with Goats Cheese

111

Halloumi
Halloumi à la Sauce Tomate ou Citron et Câpres
Halloumi Cheese with Tomato Sauce or Lemon & Caper

112

Mixed Cheeses
Fondue de Fromage avec Baguette
Cheese Fondue with a Bread Stick

114

Pâté avec Fromage au Four
Mac and Cheese

115

Roquefort
Mousse de Roquefort avec Gelée au Porto
Roquefort Mousse with Gelled Port

116

Simplicity level: ✔

Fromage Frais avec Confiture de Jalepeno

Cream Cheese with Jalepeno Jelly or Sweet Chili Jam

Presentation:
Amuse-bouche spoon for one jelly or divided dish

Ingredients:
8oz/225g Philadelphia cream cheese is traditional but a creamy goats cheese works
Jar green jalepeno jelly, red pepper jelly or the Store Cupboard sweet chili jam (see page 139)
Sherry

This amuse-bouche might appeal more to the American taste because it mixes sweet and savory. It is a fun starter for a Mexican or a Tex-Mex meal. Also, it could be served as a pre-dessert or a cheese course. It can be assembled an hour or so ahead. If you mix the red and green colors, as pictured, it makes a festive dish for the holidays.

Method:
Divide cream cheese in 8 portions and place in the spoons. You can smooth it out to fill the dish or cut a small square or rectangle. Leave enough room on top for the jelly.
In a small pan, heat 8 spoons of jelly with just enough sherry (or a little water) to thin it so it will spoon onto the cream cheese. If you are using the Store Cupboard Sweet Chili Jam, it won't be necessary to heat it before spooning it onto the cheese. Let the mixture cool a little before topping the cheese. It is nice served with a small "wheat thin" cracker if available.

Feta Marinée au Fenouil et Sésame

Fennel and Sesame marinated Feta

Presentation:
Amuse-bouche plastic or glass cubes
Cocktail sticks

Ingredients:
Small block of feta cheese
2 teaspoons of sesame seeds
1 teaspoon of fennel seeds
Grated zest of half a lemon
1 tablespoon oil
1 dessertspoon lemon juice
Fresh mint leaves
An inch of cucumber, peeled, halved and seeded
Pitted black olives, halved
A small radish per person
Black pepper

The toasted seeds enhance the marinated feta and with the bite of the cucumber and the saltiness of the olive, this makes a small mouthful of heaven! To make the brochettes easier to handle, we top each one with a small radish. You can marinate the feta beforehand and cling-filmed/plastic-wrapped, it will be fine in the fridge for up to 3 days. Assemble the brochettes up to 4 hours in advance, cover and keep cool in the fridge. Invite your guests to use the radish as a 'handle'.

Method:
Toast the seeds in a dry pan over a low heat until golden. Take care - they burn easily! Allow to cool.

Rinse and dry the feta cheese with kitchen roll and cut into half inch cubes.

Mix the lemon juice with the olive oil and a grinding of black pepper. Add the toasted seeds and mix well. Toss the feta cheese carefully in the dressing, cover and refrigerate for at least 4 hours. Take a nice, fresh sprig of mint and pull off the larger leaves for garnish. Finely chop the tiny, green leaves at the top and add to the cheese mixture.

Slice the cucumber halves into 8 thin wedges.

Thread a mint leaf, an olive half and a cucumber wedge on to the cocktail stick and finally spear a feta cube. Finish each brochette with a radish 'handle' and pop each one into an amuse-bouche cube. You can prepare these several hours before you serve them, but keep them cool in the fridge.

Mini-pizza au Chèvre

Goats Cheese Mini Pizza

Presentation:
Pretty amuse-bouche plates

Ingredients:
Roll of ready-prepared pizza
pastry
1 small goats cheese log,
thinly sliced
4 pitted black olives, halved
Paprika pepper

Store cupboard/pantry:
Fresh tomato sauce (page 134)
Chilli oil (page132)

*These pop-in-the-mouth goats cheese pizzas are served straight
from the oven (although you can prepare them ready to bake
several hours beforehand and store them in the fridge) and would
make a wonderful amuse-bouche if you have an Italian theme to
your meal. There are limitless toppings for this amuse-bouche; we
list some ideas below.*

Method:
With a pastry cutter or the rim of a sherry glass, cut out 8
small circles of pizza pastry just a little bigger than the slices
of goats cheese. Place on a sheet of baking parchment over
a wire rack or onto a non-stick pizza pan.
Spread a thin layer of fresh tomato sauce onto each
mini-pizza - but not right to the edge - and top with a slice of
goat's cheese. Put half an olive in the centre of each and
sprinkle with a little paprika. Drizzle with a little chilli oil.
You can leave these to 'rest' in the fridge for several hours if
you like.
Bake in a pre-heated oven (200 degrees C/400F) for about
10   minutes, until the goat's cheese is golden and bubbly.

Serve immediately.
Other toppings:
Spinach, mozzarella and raw
quails egg
Sautéed red pepper and
garlic
Diced chorizo, chopped rocket
and Parmesan
Crème fraiche, fine chopped
onion and bacon (omit the
tomato sauce and brush on
some olive oil instead)
Puréed black olive and
sun-dried tomato with
Parmesan.

Tomate Cerise Farcie au Chèvre

Cherry Vine Tomatoes stuffed with Goats Cheese

Cherry vine tomatoes are so attractive in the fruit bowl and are so sweet, too. Served hot with a gorgeous goats cheese stuffing and a Parmesan topping, they make a fabulous amuse bouche. We would serve these at the beginning of a vegetarian meal or after the starter between a fish and a meat course. You can prepare them the day before, and keep cool in the fridge until you're ready to cook.

Presentation:
Amuse-bouche plate, long stemmed liquor glass or amuse bouche spoon

Ingredients
8 cherry vine tomatoes
50g/2oz goats cheese
Quarter of a small red pepper, chopped finely
4 basil leaves
1 slice of yesterday's bread
2 teaspoons of finely grated Parmesan cheese
Salt & pepper
Olive oil

Method:
Pre-heat the oven to 180 degrees C/350F. Slice the 'hats' off the tomatoes with a sharp knife, complete with their stalks and retain. With a sharp knife, carefully cut out the core of each one and then scoop out the pips and juice with a small teaspoon.
Chop the goats cheese up into small pieces and mix with the red pepper and chopped basil leaves. Season. Stuff each little tomato with the mixture, pressing down firmly. Whiz the bread through the blender until you have fine breadcrumbs and then mix with the Parmesan. Season lightly.
Pile the breadcrumb mixture onto the tomatoes, pressing down to form a tiny pyramid. Drizzle with a little olive oil and pop the tomatoes onto a buttered oven-proof dish. Bake for about 8 -10 minutes

until the crumbs are golden brown. Take them out of the oven and pop on their 'hats'. Serve on a few leaves on a pretty plate.

No-cook method:
Drop the tomatoes into boiling water for a few seconds and remove. The skin should peel off easily.
At the stem end, cut an 'X' and carefully remove the seeds.
Marinate the tomatoes in a

sweet wine or sherry for at least 10 minutes, but longer if possible.
Stuff each tomato with some bought herb cheese or better still, make your own.
To serve, place the tomatoes in a long-stemmed glass and garnish with a basil leaf.
Serve with a cocktail stick.

Halloumi à la Sauce

Halloumi with Tomato Sauce

Presentation:
Amuse-bouche plate

Ingredients:
Package of Halloumi cheese
Flour optional
Butter or olive oil to coat the
bottom of the skillet
Sauce 1:
Jar of store bought salsa or
store cupboard tomato sauce
coriander/cilantro leaves -
chopped
Sauce 2:
1/2cup/110g fresh lemon juice
and 24 capers (approx)
Parsley - chopped for garnish

Halloumi is a hard middle eastern goats cheese that can be sliced and sautéed. It can be served with many accompaniments. You

Method:
Cut the cheese to the size you want but no thicker than 1/2 inch.
Dust each piece with flour (optional).
Wipe a heated non-stick skillet with oil.
Sauté the cheese pieces on both sides until browned and

soft.

Sauce 1: Warm the tomato sauce to room temperature and add the chopped coriander/cilantro leaf. Divide the sauce on the serving plates. Then place the sautéed cheese slices on top of the sauce. Garnish

s

Tomate ou Citron et Câpres

or Lemon & Caper Sauce

*can prepare these sauces ahead of time but you will need to
cook the cheese just before serving.*

with minced coriander/cilantro
leaf and serve.
Sauce 2:   Juice the lemon
and drain the capers. Set
them aside. Place the sautéed
cheese slices on the plates.
Warm the lemon juice and
capers in the skillet briefly.
Then pour on top of the
cheese. Garnish with minced

parsley and serve
immediately.

** Tip - you want enough lemon
juice so there is a little liquid on
the bottom of each dish. If you
do not have enough juice left in
your skillet you might add a
splash of white wine or olive
oil.*

amuse-bouche

Fondue de Fromage avec Baguette

Cheese Fondue with a Bread Stick

Presentation:
Amuse-bouche bowl or glass

Ingredients:
Cheese:
8oz/250g Camembert
8oz/250g Pont l'Eveque
8oz/250g Livarot
4oz/100g cream
7oz /20cl whole milk mixed with ½ teaspoon flour
Ground nutmeg to taste
2oz/4cl Calvados
Bread stick

This recipe is made with cheeses from Normandy but you could substitute with less expensive or perhaps easier to find cheeses in your area. Rich flavored cheeses are the best and the amount of each can vary. The French often combine whatever leftover bits of cheese they have. The bread sticks can be made a day ahead and stored in a plastic sack. An Alsatian wine or a Pinot Noir is a nice accompaniment.

Method:
Cut bread sticks from a white or pumpernickel loaf to a 1 inch square and a length to fit your serving dish. Let them dry on the counter or place them on an oven tray and dry in a very low oven. Brush with melted garlic butter and brown in a moderate oven, or sauté. These toasted sticks can be prepared ahead of time.
Cut the rind off the cheese and discard. Dice the cheese. Mix the flour with the milk and heat in a nonstick saucepan on low. Add the cheeses. When melted, add cream and nutmeg. Bring to a simmer. Add the Calvados and transfer to your amuse-bouche serving dish. Garnish with a bread stick and serve warm.

Paté avec Fromage au Four

Mac and Cheese

Presentation:
Amuse-bouche gratin dish

Ingredients:
8oz/250ml small elbow macaroni or coquillette (a miniature macaroni)
¾ cup/190ml cream
2tbsp butter
Salt and pepper
¾ cup/190ml cheese - assortment of sharp cheddar, old Gouda, Gruyere and Emmenthal
Paprika for garnish
Breadcrumbs (optional) - fine ground

"Mac and Cheese" is an American staple. Most kids live on it while growing up and the sense of it being a comfort food exists well into adulthood. Serving it as an amuse-bouche should bring a chuckle to your dinner table. You can prepare the dishes beforehand and pop them into the oven 10 -15 minutes before serving.

Method:
Heat oven to 400F/200C
Parboil the macaroni in salted water until 'al dente'. Drain.
Make a sauce by heating the butter, cream, salt, pepper, paprika and cheeses until melted together (the sauce should have a solid cheesy flavor.)
Mix the macaroni into the cheese sauce and spoon into your overproof serving dishes. Top with bread crumbs drizzled with butter or a little shredded cheese.

Bake until the crumbs are browned or the is cheese melted.

Mousse de Roquefort avec Gelèe au Porto

Roquefort Mousse with Gelled Port

Presentation:
Amuse-bouche glass

Ingredients:
8oz/250ml ruby Port
2Tbs/30ml powdered gelatine
or 1 sheet gelatin
4 oz/110g Roquefort cheese
½cup/125ml cream
Chives for garnish

A glass shows off the colors of this amuse-bouche. The Roquefort is not overpowering in flavor as it is whipped with the cream and the sweetness of the ruby Port is meant for a strong cheese. Chill in the refrigerator until ready to serve. This can be done a day ahead and assures that the Port has gelled. Remember that all gelatins are not the same so follow directions on your package.

Method:
Mix the Port and gelatine according to the directions on the gelatin package. It should gel but not be solid - a soft gel.
Place in the bottom of your serving glass and chill, ideally for 24 hours.
In a small bowl, whip the cheese, adding the cream as you go. It should not be runny but light and fluffy and hold its form.
Spoon or pipe the cheese on top of the gelled Port.
Garnish with chives.

Sucré
Desserts

Banane Sautée

Sautéed Banana

Presentation:
Amuse-bouche spoon

Ingredients:
8 banana slices - 1/2 inch thick
2 or 3 graham crackers/
digestive biscuits, finely
crumbled
Coriander/cilantro leaf minced
to taste
1tblsp/15ml butter for sauté
8 mint leaves
8tsp/5ml crème fraiche or
yoghurt

This tidbit could be served as an amuse-bouche before an Asian meal or as a pre-dessert. A plain sweet biscuit or cookie can be substituted for the graham crackers which are popular for making crumb crusts in the United States.

Method:
Put the graham crackers or cookies between 2 pieces baking paper and roll with a rolling pin.

Mince the coriander/cilantro and mix with the cracker crumbs.
Dip both sides of the banana slices in the mixture and sauté in butter until warm and golden.
Put crème fraiche or yogurt in the bottom of a serving spoon and top with a banana slice. Garnish with a small mint leaf and serve straight away.

Café Gourmand

Luxury Coffee Plate

Presentation:
A large flat serving platter per person, a pretty little coffee cup and amuse-bouche dishes and verrines

Café Gourmand is becoming very popular in restaurants in France and replaces the normal dessert course. A shot of dark, bitter espresso is served with a selection of little cakes and sucrées on a single plate. You could use any of the amuse-bouches sucrées in this book to make up your plate, or a selection of your own. In our picture, we have used Baby Meringues, Strawberry and Lemon Cheesecake slices, a Petit Pot of Chocolate 'Guinness' and a Dark Chocolate, Pistachio and Cherry layered verrine. You can make up the desserts beforehand but don't 'sandwich' the meringues or make the cheescakes too far in advance or else they will go soggy.

Method:
For the meringues, fold 60g/2½oz caster sugar into a whipped egg white, spoon teaspoons of the mixture onto baking parchment and bake for an hour at 140C/275F. Turn the oven off and leave them to dry out in the oven until they are completely cold. Sandwich with whipped cream just before serving.
Continued on pages 120 -121

Café Gourmand

Luxury Coffee Plate

For the cheesecakes, make tiny, individual cheesecakes using 60g/2½oz crushed digestive biscuits/graham crackers with 25g/1oz butter for the base. If you line your moulds with clingfilm/plastic wrap, they will be easier to turn out. Allow to set in the fridge and then prepare the filling, using an egg yolk, 30g/1¼oz caster sugar and a Petit Suisse or cream cheese. Whiz in the blender with a melted gelatine leaf and then add 75ml/3fl oz of whipped double cream. Tip the mixture onto the base of each cheesecake and chill for 3 hours before turning out. Garnish with lemon and strawberries.

For the chocolate pot, whisk 2 egg whites and then fold in 4 teaspoons of golden caster sugar. Melt 120g/5oz of dark chocolate in a bowl over hot water, cool and then stir it into the egg yolks (optional). Fold the egg whites into the chocolate mixture. Chill for at least 3 hours and then top with whipped cream.

For the chocolate, pistachio and cherry layered verrine, use layers of thick yoghurt, shop-bought chocolate and pistachio puddings ('Paturages' desserts from French supermarkets are very good) and top with a tablespoon of fresh fruit compote.

Café Gourmand

Luxury Coffee Plate

Another favourite for a Café Gormand plate is a Chestnut Puree with Crème Fraiche verrine - open a can of sweetened chestnut puree, put a teaspoon or two into a verrine and top with crème fraiche - or you could layer it, as above. Garnish with a mint leaf.

Or make some tiny profiteroles - boil 150ml/5fl oz of water with 50g/2oz of butter, remove from the heat and 'shoot' in 60g/2½oz of plain flour. Beat vigorously with a wooden spoon to form a smooth ball of pastry and then add a beaten egg, a little at a time, until you have a firm smooth paste. Bake teaspoons of the mixture on a greased tray for 20-25 minutes at 190 degrees C/375F until they are gold and puffy. Cool on a wire rack, then using a cream aerosol, fill them with whipped cream and finally top with coffee or chocolate icing.

Arrange a meringue, cheesecake, chocolate pot, profiterole and verrine (or any of the other sucreés in this book) on each platter. Then make some strong black Espresso coffee and add a cup of this to the platters before serving with a small coffee spoon.

Diplomate au Gingembre
Ginger Trifle

Presentation:
Port glass or verrine

Ingredients:
Box of almond biscuits/cookies or gingernuts/ginger snaps
Carton of thick creamy vanilla custard/crème Anglaise
Jar of good quality strawberry jam (homemade if possible)
Stones Ginger Wine
Jar of Chinese Stem Ginger
Aerosol of cream or fresh whipped cream
Toasted flaked almonds to garnish

Everyone loves a trifle and this is simplicity itself to prepare. We first served this at a summer barbeque and it was very popular. Since then, the addition of Chinese stem ginger has made it even more special. You can prepare these little sucrées the day before, chill them in the fridge and top with cream and almond flakes just before serving.

Method:
Put an almond biscuit in the base of each glass - break it up to fit, if necessary. If you are using gingernuts instead, you might like to add a few toasted flaked almonds. Chop the ginger into tiny pieces and put a few pieces into each glass. Pour enough ginger wine to cover the biscuit and allow it to soak up the wine for 5 minutes or so. Soften the strawberry jam if necessary and put a teaspoon into each verrine. Top each one with enough custard to cover the jam. Chill until ready to serve. Just before you do, decorate the top of the trifle with the whipped cream and scatter over a few toasted almonds.

'Gari' Glace au Gingembre
Gingernut Ice Cream with Pickled Ginger

How can a simple ice-cream taste so spectacular! The sweetness and the crunch of the gingernut ice cream complements the sharpness of the Gari and the result is a mouthful of heaven.

Presentation:
Tall sundae glasses or verrines

Ingredients:
Half a litre/pint of good vanilla ice-cream
4 gingernut biscuits or ginger snaps
1 dessertspoon thick honey
A little grated white chocolate

Store Cupboard:
6 small teaspoons of Gari (pickled ginger - see page 135)

Method:
Put the ice-cream into a bowl and allow to soften for 5 minutes or so. Meanwhile, crush the biscuits between some baking parchment with a rolling-pin. Don't reduce to 'breadcrumbs' - you need to retain a crunch. Lightly mix the biscuits into the ice-cream with the honey, cover and return to the freezer to set. When you're ready to serve, put a little gari with some juice into the bottom of your sundae glasses. Using an ice-cream scoop (it helps if you wet it in luke-warm water to start with) put a ball of ice-cream on top of the gari. Sprinkle with grated white chocolate and serve straight away.

Gelée d'Orange et Cointreau

Orange & Cointreau Jelly

Presentation:
Port glass, verrine or champagne flute

Ingredients:
2 sheets of leaf gelatine
2 oranges
260 ml/½ pint freshly squeezed orange juice
60g/2½oz caster sugar
1 tablespoon Cointreau
2 tablespoons ricotta cheese
2 tablespoons crème fraiche
2 teaspoons caster sugar
Juice of half a lemon
Grated white chocolate or cherry compote to garnish

This fresh orange, tangy jelly with a lemon cheese mousse topping should be served before your dessert course and your guests will be begging for more! Served in a tiny Port glass like this, it is the perfect 'aperitif' to a delicious summer pudding. For a change, use a taller, champagne flute and top with fresh fruit compote of your choice; we used black cherry, which worked well

Method:
Soften the gelatine in a small bowl of cold water.
Peel the oranges with a knife to remove peel and pith. Separate the segments and remove the membranes. Cut the orange flesh into small pieces and put a couple into the base of each verrine.
Heat the orange juice with the sugar, stirring until it has dissolved. Remove from the heat and add the softened gelatine, stir thoroughly until completely dissolved. Add the Cointreau. Pour the warm mixture over the orange segments, leaving a space for the mousse, and chill for at least 4 hours.
To make the mousse, whip the ricotta with the crème fraiche, caster sugar and lemon juice. When the jelly has set, fill each verrine to the top with the mousse. Return to the fridge to set. Serve with a little grated white chocolate or other decoration.

For a change, use a small champagne flute instead of the verrine and when the mousse has set, top with a teaspoon or two of cherry compote.

avec Mousse de Ricotta

with Ricotta Mousse

Glace à la Vanille avec de Mangue et Sirop Fruit de la Passion

Vanilla Ice Cream with Mango and Passion Fruit Liqueur

This refreshing pre-dessert has the taste of the tropics. You can peel and dice the mango beforehand and chill until you are ready to prepare the verrines.

Presentation:
Amuse-bouche glass/verrine

Ingredients:
8 small balls of vanilla ice cream
8 cubes of mango - fresh or canned
8oz/250ml Passoa - a liqueur made from passion fruits or another compatible fruit liqueur
8 mint leaf to garnish

Method:
Small dice the mango. Place a small scoop of vanilla ice cream in each serving glass and top with a cube of mango. Gently ladle liqueur over the top. Garnish with a mint leaf.

Tarte à la Rhubarbe

Rhubarb Tart

This is an almost fool-proof pre-dessert and it can be made a day ahead. For ease, use a store-bought pastry dough, preferably one that is pre-rolled and ready to put in your miniature tart moulds. Cut the dough in rounds to fit your moulds or you can use the bottom of a muffin tin. When cutting the individual rounds, allow enough dough to go up the sides of the muffin tin about one inch. Place baking paper in bottom of the moulds for easy removal of the tarts.

Presentation:
Amuse-bouche plate

Ingredients:
2 cups/256g fresh rhubarb chopped small
6 oz/150g granulated sugar
2oz/56g flour
1oz/ 28g butter
1pre-made tart pastry

Method:
Preheat oven to 400F/200C.
Fine chop the rhubarb and place it in a mixing bowl.
Mix the sugar and flour, add the rhubarb and toss well.
Let the mixture sit for about 20 minutes.
Cut 8 rounds (the size to fit your baking dish) out of the tart pastry.
Use non-stick baking tins or line the bottom with baking paper
Place a pastry round in each dish.
Fill with the rhubarb mixture, dot with butter and bake for about half an hour. Remove from the tin and serve warm.

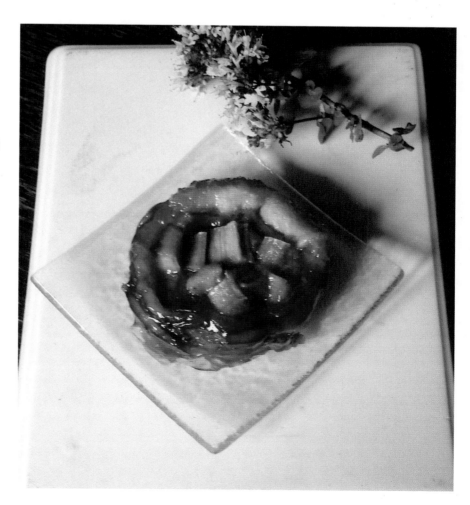

Panna Cotta aux

Panna Cotta with Raspberry

Presentation:
Amuse-bouche plate or verrine

Ingredients:
2 cups/½ litre heavy cream or half and half
¼ cup/50g sugar
1 teaspoons of vanilla extract
1 packets powdered gelatine about (2¼ teaspoons) or
13g of sheet gelatin
3 tablespoons/45ml cold water
Raspberry sauce
Jar of caramel or chocolate sauce

This Italian inspired recipe is used as a pre-dessert or part of a

Method:
Heat the cream and sugar in a saucepan or microwave. Once the sugar is dissolved, remove from heat and stir in vanilla extract.
Sprinkle powdered gelatine over the cold water in a medium size bowl and let stand for 5-10 minutes. If you are using sheet gelatine, soften it in water and wring out the water with your hands. Then pour the very warm Panna Cotta mix over the gelatine and stir until the gelatine is completely dissolved.
If you plan to unmould the Panna Cotta, lightly oil the containers with a neutral tasting oil.

Framboises ou au Caramel

or Caramel

Café Gourmand. It is very easy to make and can be made a couple days ahead. Cover tightly and chill.

Divide the mixture into the prepared dishes and chill until firm (2-4 hours minimum). Run a sharp knife around the edge of Panna Cotta to unmould or serve in a verrine with your favorite topping. Top with a store bought raspberry sauce garnished with a fresh raspberry or to make your own sauce, put fresh raspberries in a bowl and add sugar to your taste. Let them sit for an hour then pass through a food mill to obtain a smooth sauce.

Alternatively, purchase a caramel or chocolate sauce (for a different flavored chocolate sauce you can add some maple syrup and/or rum).

Saumon Fumé sur Crème du Concombre - see page 72

Store Cupboard/Pantry Recipes

Chilli Oil

Ingredients:
Extra virgin olive oil
I large fresh chilli or an
assortment of smaller yellow &
red chillis
Dried chilli flakes
Black pepper

This fiery oil is simplicity itself but is so useful to spice up all sorts of things, including our Mini-pizza au Chèvre pizzas (see page 110). Make up a jar and it will keep in the store cupboard for months. Keep topping it up with oil as you use it, and add a few chilli flakes from time to time.

Method:
Pop your chilli, stalk and all, into a sterilized, screw-top jar. Add half a teaspoon of dried chilli flakes (or more if you really like it hot!), grind in some black pepper and then fill the jar to the top with olive oil The chilli should be covered. Replace the top on the jar and give it a good shake. This will improve with age so make it well ahead of time.

Cumberland Jelly

This wonderful, sharp, spicy jelly goes well with our Foie de Volaille amuse-bouche (see page 90). It will last in a sterilised, screw-top jar in the fridge for several months. Beware, though, it melts if left out for any length of time so always serve straight from the fridge.

Ingredients:
3 sheets of gelatine
Juice of a lemon
Juice of an orange
4 tablespoons redcurrant jelly
4 tablespoons Port
1 heaped teaspoon of English mustard powder
I heaped teaspoon of ground ginger

Method:
Soften the gelatine sheets in a bowl of cold water for 5 minutes. Mix the mustard powder and ground ginger to a paste with a little of the lemon juice. Gradually add the rest of the lemon juice, the orange juice and the Port.

Melt the redcurrant jelly in a pan over a low heat, and then add the gelatine sheets. Stir until dissolved and then add the mustard mixture. Pour the jelly into a jar and allow to set for a couple of hours in the fridge before use.

Simplicity level: ✓ ✓

Fresh Tomato Sauce

Ingredients:
1 tablespoon olive oil
1 onion, finely chopped
3 cloves garlic, crushed
1 teaspoons of tomato purée
500g/1 lb fresh tomatoes
roughly chopped or a
450g/14 oz tin of tomatoes
1 teaspoon of sugar
2 teaspoons of fresh thyme
leaves
Salt & pepper

Make up a batch of this when tomatoes are cheap or you have a surplus from the garden, or use a can. Covered, it will keep fresh in the fridge for a week or so but it is better to freeze the mixture in small plastic pots so that you can use it 'fresh' each time. It is a perfect base for so many tarts and sauces.

Method:
Heat the oil in a large pan and cook the onions and garlic over a medium heat for 5 minutes or so until soft and golden. Stir occasionally and avoid browning. Add the tomato purée and cook for a further minute. Add the chopped tomatoes, sugar and thyme and simmer gently for 20-25 minutes until the tomatoes are soft. Blend in a food processor and season to taste.

Gari (pickled ginger)

Delicious with our Gari Glace au Gingembre (see page 122), this is traditionally served with sushi (see page 38). It's very simple to make but it's best made at least 3 or 4 days before you want to use it. It will keep in the fridge forever, and will gradually turn pink as it matures.

Ingredients:
250g/9 oz root ginger
90 ml/3½ fl oz rice vinegar
2 tablespoons caster sugar
2 tablespoons sweet white wine or saki rice wine

Method:
Peel the ginger and blanch it in boiling water for 1 minute. Allow to cool and chop it up fairly finely.
Mix the other ingredients together in a pan and stir over a low heat until the sugar has dissolved. Bring to the boil and let it bubble for a few minutes. Cool.
Put the chopped ginger into a sterilised screw-top jar and cover with the liquid.

Simplicity level: ✔

Onion Marmalade

Ingredients:
700g/1½ lbs large onions, peeled and chopped finely
600g/1lb 5oz sugar
300ml/½ pint white wine vinegar
3 teaspoons of caraway seeds
1 teaspoon salt

Onion marmalade is absolutely perfect with foie gras. We use it in our Croutons au Foie Gras amuse-bouche on page 98. We always have a jar or two of this in our store cupboard and it lasts as long as normal marmalade. Don't be tempted to leave out the caraway seeds; they really make this marmalade special.

Method:
Put the sugar and vinegar into a large saucepan on a gentle heat and stirring, cook for about 5 minutes until all the sugar has dissolved.
Add the chopped onions, caraway seeds and salt, bring to the boil, then turn the heat down and simmer for about two hours until the syrup is thick. Pour into sterilised, screw-top jars.

Pesto Mayonnaise

This is a very rich mayonnaise and is quite delicious as a dipping sauce for prawns or raw vegetables. It will keep in the fridge for about 3 days in a screw top jar, or a small bowl, covered with plastic wrap/clingfilm.

Method:
Using your blender, whiz the egg yolks, adding a little oil at a time. When it emulsifies, add the rest of the oil in a steady stream. Add the lemon juice, and scrape the mayonnaise into a bowl.

Put the basil leaves, garlic, pine nuts and cheese into the blender and add a little more oil. Whiz until smooth. Add the mixture to the mayonnaise and stir well. Season to taste. Cover and chill.

Ingredients:
2 egg yolks
2 tablespoons of olive oil
1 dessertspoon fresh lemon juice
Large handful of fresh basil leaves
1 clove garlic
1 tablespoon pine nuts
1 tablespoon grated Parmesan cheese
Salt & pepper

Pesto

The pesto recipe can be used in many dishes and can be made ahead and chilled or frozen. It is good with pastas, tomatoes and cheeses

Method:
Place basil and garlic (cut in half) in the bowl of a food processor and chop. While the processor is running, dribble in the oil through the feed tube. When well blended, add the Parmesan, pine nuts and salt. Pulse until well mixed. Transfer to a storage container. In the fridge, it will keep a week or two if you cover the top with a layer of olive oil. For long conservation, it will keep for several months frozen.

Ingredients:
1½cup/375ml basil leaves
2-3 cloves of garlic
2/3cup/170ml olive oil
½cup/125ml grated Parmesan
½cup/125ml pine nuts
Coarse salt to taste - a big pinch

Sauce Aigre-douce

Ingredients:
5 slices of pineapple (fresh or canned) and its juice
1 small green pepper, de-seeded and diced
1 level dessertspoon of corn flour/starch
1 dessertspoon of soya sauce
3 dessertspoons of white wine vinegar
30g/2oz of caster sugar

This simple-to-make sweet and sour pineapple sauce can be stored in a screw-top jar in the fridge for a week or two - although it's unlikely to stay in our fridge for that long it's so good! Serve with samosas (see page 93) or any spicy food.

Method:
Cut the top off the pineapple and extract the flesh, using a pineapple cutter or a sharp knife over a plate to catch the juices, leaving behind the skin and the core. Chop the flesh into tiny pieces.
Pour the juice into a saucepan and add the sugar, vinegar and soya sauce. Stir over a gentle heat until the sugar has melted.
Mix the corn flour with a little water and stir it into the mixture. Bring gently to the boil, stirring until thickened. Add the pineapple pieces and the diced green pepper and bring back to the boil, stirring to prevent it burning. Remove from the heat.
Use a stick blender to reduce the size of the pineapple and pepper but don't blend until smooth - it should be a little lumpy.
Pour into a sterilised screw-top jar and store in the fridge.

Sweet Chilli Jam

This ruby-red, sweet but fiery sauce looks spectacular and tastes good with most cold meats and quiches - or anything wrapped in filo pastry. It will keep in the store cupboard for many months, but it is advisable to refrigerate once you have opened the jar.

Ingredients
500g/1lb 2oz sugar
600ml/1 pint water
3 cloves of garlic, roughly chopped
A knob of ginger, peeled and chopped
8 red chillies*, stalks removed and roughly chopped
2 tablespoons of fish sauce
410g/14oz can chopped tomatoes
Dried chilli flakes (optional)

Method
Dissolve the sugar and water together over a low heat, stirring until the sugar has completely dissolved. Add the fish sauce and tinned tomatoes and mix well. Next add the chopped chillies, seeds and all, and finally the chopped ginger and garlic. Bring to the boil, stir well and then reduce the heat and simmer for 30 minutes or until the mixture has reduced by about half. The sauce should coat the back of a spoon. Allow to cool a little and taste. Add a few chilli flakes to spice it up if you like. Blend the mixture in a processor and pour into sterilised, screw-topped jars.

* Also spelt chili, the chillies used in this recipe are the small, red hot-tasting pods often used in Mexican dishes, such as chilli con carne

'Sun-dried' Tomatoes

Ingredients:
Ripe tomatoes without stalks
Olive oil
Salt

Whenever we have a glut of tomatoes in the garden, we make our own 'sun-dried' tomatoes - in the oven! They are so delicious and will keep in sterilised jars for at least a year.

Method:
Turn the oven to its lowest setting.
Cut the tomatoes in half from top to bottom. Lay them out on wire cooling trays, which you will slide onto the oven racks. They shouldn't touch. Season them lightly with salt. Cook for up to 12 hours, or overnight. They should dry out completely but remain flexible, not brittle. Let them cool completely on the wire racks before packing them into sterilised, screw top jars. Cover completely with olive oil and seal. They improve with age, so think ahead.

Fig Chutney

In our part of France, most gardens have a fig tree and in September, there is usually a glut. We usually make this delicious chutney which is so good served with Foie Gras or duck, as well as cold meats, at about this time. You can buy figs at most grocery stores in September/October and this is the time to make this chutney. If you have to pay for them, you may want to cut the ingredients down by half. The chutney will last for at least six months in the store cupboard but refrigerate once the jar is opened.

Ingredients (makes about 4 large jars)
About 26-30 plump fresh figs
275 ml/1/2 pint balsamic vinegar
200 ml/4 fl oz red wine vinegar
600g/1lb 5oz soft brown sugar
Zest and juice of a lemon
4 red onions, finely sliced
4 teaspoons mixed spice
Large knob of fresh ginger, grated
2 tablespoons of olive oil
Salt & pepper

Method
Heat the oil in a large, heavy bottomed pan and add the onions. Gently fry the onions for about 5-10 minutes until soft and translucent.
Add all the other ingredients except for the figs and season with salt and pepper. Bring to the boil and then turn the heat down and simmer for 30 minutes or until the mixture is reduced to a syrup.
Meanwhile, remove the stalks from the figs and cut them into quarters. When your mixture is ready, add the figs and cook for another 15 minutes, stirring occasionally.
Remove from the heat and carefully ladle the mixture into sterilised, screw-topped jars.

Index

White Bean Purée, page 32

amuse-bouche

Gingernut Ice Cream with Pickled Ginger Page 123

Mango with Scallops, page 74

*Asparagus, Avocado and
Shrimp/Prawn Salad, page 77*

Index

Sorbet

Spinach

Squash

Strawberry

Sun-dried Tomatoes

Sweet peppers

Tomato

Tuna

Yam

Yam Purée with Ginger, Page 42

Sushi Rice Balls with Wasabi Cucumber page 38

amuse-bouche

Printed in Great Britain
by Amazon.co.uk, Ltd.,
Marston Gate.